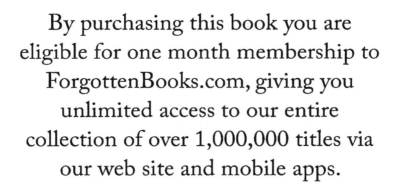

ISBN 978-0-260-02513-5
PIBN 10923018

This book is a reproduction of an important historical work. Forgotten Books uses
state-of-the-art technology to digitally reconstruct the work, preserving the original format
whilst repairing imperfections present in the aged copy. In rare cases, an imperfection in
the original, such as a blemish or missing page, may be replicated in our edition. We do,
however, repair the vast majority of imperfections successfully; any imperfections that
remain are intentionally left to preserve the state of such historical works.

OBERLIN
ALUMNI
MAGAZINE

DECEMBER, 1932

VOLUME XXIX

NUMBER 3

Section of the chart "American Business Activity Since 1790" prepared originally by Col. Leonard P. Ayres, Vice President of The Cleveland Trust Company

1894 1932

SILVER CAMPAIGN DEPRESSION

RECOVERY OF 1895

MERGER PROSPERITY

CORPORATE PROSPERITY

RICH MAN'S PANIC

PANIC OF 1907

WAR DEPRESSION

WAR PROSPERITY

POST WAR DEPRESSION

COOLIDGE PROSPERITY

DEPRESSION OF THE 30'S

PENDULUMS
work that way

THE swing of the pendulum is in response to a law of nature, and it applies to business.

This bank has seen many economic storms come and go—and each time the pendulum has swung back to reconstruction and recovery. Always this has been accompanied by increased economy, greater efficiency, by simplicity, self-denial and courage.

We emerge each time with deeper experience and stronger faith in the soundness of the fundamental policies that survive all phases of the business cycle.

To sound businesses whose policies have likewise stood the test, this bank since its organization in 1894, has lent its cooperation and support and will continue to do so.

Cleveland Trust
Member Federal Reserve System

THE OBERLIN ALUMNI MAGAZINE

Published Monthly, Except in August and September by
THE ALUMNI ASSOCIATION OF OBERLIN COLLEGE

EXECUTIVE COMMITTEE

President—Frank C. VanCleef, '04
First Vice-President—Mrs. Louise A. Nichols, '11
Second Vice-President—Theodore H. Harvey, '10
Recording Secretary—Mabel J. Baker, '12
Treasurer—J. Clement Boyers, '07
Mrs. Esther R. Bowen, '11
R. T. Miller, Jr., '91
Chairman, Alumnae Affiliation Committee—
Mrs. Agnes W. Mastick, '92

EDITOR ALUMNI MAGAZINE
Dorothy Hall, '27
Assistant, Evelyn V. Latham, '29

Alumni Association Membership, $2.50 per year
Alumni Magazine Subscription, $2.50 per year
Single copies, 25 cents

Should a subscriber desire to discontinue his subscription, a notice to the effect should be sent in before its expiration. Otherwise it is assumed that a continuance of the subscription is desired.

Communications and advertising copy should be in hand by the 15th of the month to insure attention for the next issue.

Draw checks to The Alumni Association of Oberlin College.

Member, American Alumni Council, Intercollegiate Alumni Extension Service, Inc.

Entered as second-class matter at the Post Office, Oberlin, Ohio, under Act of Congress of March 3, 1879.

Gifts and Wishes

What sort of Christmas does Oberlin want, and what "best" wishes for the new year?

FOR HERSELF she wishes: that she may in this year not fall below her past; that she may hold firm her determination never to be a spiritual onlooker, but to take effective part on the side of the as-nearly-right as she can conceive. She accepts as her greatest gift the responsibility of the lives in her charge, and her unique opportunity to be to them stimulating and formative.

FOR HER STUDENTS she wishes honesty of mind; and, along with a true perspective on themselves and the world, essential seriousness in dealing with life. She wishes that she may give them some glimpse of the harmonious world of knowledge; that, becoming aware of vast patterns in the universe, they may feel at home there and capable, not isolated and helpless. She wishes that she may be able to teach them how to spend wisely their divine gift of discontent. Above all she wishes for them the two lost gifts of the twentieth century—leadership and nobility.

FOR HER GRADUATES she wishes gifts of the good life—peace, courage, humor and love. She wishes that she may always be bound to them, and they to her, in the fellowship of the *attainable good life*—the simplicity, integrity and openness of spirit that in quiet, rises before the mind as a revelation of the natural way to live.

6c

The Oberlin Alumni Magazine

VOLUME XXIX OBERLIN, OHIO, DECEMBER 1, 1932 No. 3

In this "tough-minded" age, when we are bidden to cast sentimental attachments and other such-like impedimenta onto the Victorian dust-heap, when saints are shorn of their haloes and great men of their glory, when the prevailing idea seems to be a clean break with the past, including any unpleasant consequences of our own past acts—in this year of grace, in short—it may fairly be asked: Are not alumni obsolete? Why should any modern college, turning out sanitary, germ-free products, wrapped in intellectual cellophane, need to know what happens to its little packages once out in the world? The brooder's superiority to the hen lies precisely in the fact that it specializes in brooding. Scratching for its chicks, concern about their welfare, it leaves to others. Why not the college likewise?

WHY DOES OBERLIN NEED ALUMNI?

Why does Oberlin want and need active and interested alumni? What does she get from them?

Two points occur immediately, a third a second after. They are, in order, money, students, prestige.

A college feels as a matter of course that when real need of *money* arises, either for necessary endowment or to weather some financial crisis, its alumni, and not strangers, constitute the natural court of appeal. And to a great extent it is alumni and alumni connections, who feel interested enough in any institution to furnish the funds that make its program possible.

Further, a college needs *students*; alumni have every reason, from the college's point of view, to wish their children to drink from the fountain-head that quenched their thirst.

Still further, a distinguished and active alumni body advertises the college as nothing else can—interests other people's children, deflects other people's money into the college coffers; contributes that cash asset known variously as *"reputation"* and "good-will." An educational institution indeed receives more than purely material returns from a high reputation; it reaps also an accession of confidence and a stiffening of morale. These are some of the more tangible values accruing to a college through its alumni.

And there are still other values to be derived from an alumni body. There is *continuity of tradition*, which comes from teaching sons and sons of sons, and sons of them again; daughters and daughters of daughters. The presence in an alumni body of family continuities is like a long fiber in a fabric. It gives strength and stability to the whole.

Alumni opinion, when it is prompted by genuine love and gratitude, and when it is an intelligent commentary on the college as it is and not a vague remembrance of "in my day"—enlightened alumni opinion, representing the outside point-of-view, is one of the greatest assets a college may have. The alumnus may become the share-holder, the associate, in the college adventure.

It is good, moreover, for all human enterprises to move in an atmosphere of understanding and love. Science, the incorruptible, rules out love from its laboratories—except, perhaps, the love of truth; it is prone to forget, sometimes, that the antiseptic solution is also sterile. In human relationships, at any rate, mind without heart is sterile—it must be mind and heart, or nothing is accomplished.

Oberlin *needs* its alumni, now and increasingly. It needs them for the stimulus of an outside point-of-view, for reputation, for students, for continuity; for money, and for love.

Whatever its concealed cleverness as a political move may be, to the innocent lay mind seeking a symbol of better hopes President Hoover's invitation to President-elect Roosevelt to discuss with him the foreign debt situation seems a distinct step forward. It is, ever so faintly, an intrusion of rational idealism and good sense into politics, a hint that perhaps in the millenium, Government may come before Party.

FALSE DAWN?

The history of party, in the United States, has never been so very noble. Whatever their quiet little working agreements may have been, some honorable and some not quite so honorable, the Republicans and Democrats have taken care that they shall be perennially cat and dog in the public mind. Truth, good sense, the end of Government itself, have been subordinated to this. It may be argued that Republicans, in power, have appropriated workable Democratic ideas under their own name and signet, and the Democrats in a similar situation have done the same by the Republicans. It may be true, probably is true; and as regards what we have actually got, or not got, out of either party, we the people have hardly been the loser. But the people *have* been the loser, in a very real sense, to have had this false distinction twixt Tweedledum and Tweedledee drilled into them from their cradles. It has made their political thinking puerile; it has made them susceptible to any sort of election ballyhoo; it has made them not only incredulous, but incapable, of imagining anything like fair play or sportsmanship or collaboration *between* parties.

And there is another faint ray of hope. It is gratifying to Oberlin, of course, to have touched even briefly the life and thinking of Dr. Raymond Moley, the professor of Columbia who attended Governor Roosevelt as consultant and adviser. It is even more gratifying to see a politician at least listening to the opinions of a man who is supposed to be dedicated not to Party but to the truth. No spectacle has been more disquieting to educators (and rightfully so), than that of professional, impartial observers of fact shut up into laboratories and college lecture rooms, while the politicians, blissfully unaware of it all, ran the nation. It indicated a ghastly discrepancy somewhere, either a failure on the part of colleges and

(Continued on page 78)

Some Impressions of Soviet Russia

BY PROFESSOR NEWELL L. SIMS*

I AM told that one who enters Russia from the Orient sees it as the frontier of the West and the beginnings of the twentieth century; but he who approaches from the west, as I did, beholds in it the outpost of the Orient and the end of the middle ages. However, first impressions quickly yield to more discriminating ones as the traveler becomes aware of the striking contrasts that exist in this land.

To be sure there are contrasts in every land, but in the Soviet Republics one surely encounters them in wider ranges of life and on a greater scale than anywhere else on the globe today. This is due to the fact that Russia is changing. The old is being replaced by the new more fundamentally, more extensively and more rapidly than it has ever been at any time or place in human history. The visitor to Russia witnesses the modern wonder of the world.

As you see revolution in process throughout the length, and breadth of the land, you soon perceive that the fateful events of November 6 and 7, 1917, were only the beginnings of a movement which continues to this hour, and which will persist for at least another generation. The impression of transformation, alteration, reconstruction, uprooting and replanting, attended with much confusion and chaos and presided over by a master plan and purpose. is an inescapable one. These changes appear to the westerner almost incredible—indeed, all but impossible. In the words of Romain Rolland, they represent "the most necessary work of the century," at least for Russia.

The most conspicuous thing confronting the visitor to the U. S. S. R. is the industrial revolution. The building of factories and plants is everywhere to be seen. Rapidly expanding cities and "boom" towns give concrete evidence of the development of some of the greatest enterprises men have ever attempted. When, therefore, you see vast new manufacturing centers springing like magic in an incredibly short time out of nothingness and waste, you begin to appreciate the reality and the magnitude of Soviet achievement.

Under a planned economy and by sacrifice unprecedented the U. S. S. R. is attempting in a decade or so to convert an agricultural country into a manufacturing country—a process that it took a century to accomplish in England and Germany. The audacity of the idea, however, is no more impressive than the evidences of its steady realization. Since the inception of the five-year plan over seven hundred new industrial plants have been built, and in this the fourth year of the plan's operation it has been so far fulfilled that a second five-year plan has been launched. In 1932 alone, eleven billions of dollars of new capital, representing forty percent of the national income, have been invested. In the United States with four times the income we save not over fif-

teen percent for investment. Thus one gets some idea of the sacrifice the Soviets are making to build industry; and if they are able to keep it up for a few years there is little reason to doubt that their dream will be accomplished not much behind schedule.

Although less spectacular than the industrial changes, the agrarian revolution impressed me as being more significant and daring and even more sweeping. When you discover that the state farms now operating cover an area larger than all Germany, and find that three times as many farmers as we have in all America, or about two-thirds of all the peasants of Russia, are embraced in the collectives of the Soviet Union, it is something to awaken more than passing interest. Socialistic agriculture actually predominates today, produces four-fifths of the crops and steadily moves toward the complete elimination of individualistic farming. The growth of collective farming is due to its inherent advantages under the Soviet system. It makes possible the cultivation of more land, increases production, gives the peasant many things he never before enjoyed and promises a standard of living not hitherto attained. Although there are many difficult problems yet unsolved, which only the experience of a generation can cure, it is at once apparent that socialistic agriculture is sufficiently well established and is already enough of a success to give it every mark of permanency. Of this fact I was doubtful until I saw for myself.

The most voracious observer ought to be satisfied with the sight of two revolutions going on simultaneously, but Russia is a land of extremes and does not let you off so easily. It has a third revolution in operation: a psychological one. This upheaval is the greatest of all and the one that impressed me most, for while other lands have built industry and reorganized agriculture, none has undergone such a profound change of mind as is taking place in this nation. You do not exactly see it so much as you sense it. But if you penetrate below a surface efflorescent with material construction and reorganization, you come upon a soul in process of alteration. The old magical, lackadaisical, individualistic, capitalistic, "dark mind" is giving way to a new assertive, rationalized, socialized, humanized and hopeful mind. The new conditions are inducing it and it in turn is providing a secure foundation for the new order.

It is difficult in the brief space allotted me to convey any adequate notion of the part played by the new attitudes, new motives, new values and new views of life as I sensed them among the Russians. Perhaps a few inklings of these can be suggested from some of my contacts with the citizens of the cities and steppes of the U. S. S. R.

The new attitude toward labor which one detects in the factories, among the party members everywhere and especially among the youth, is wholesome. Labor is praised as the noblest thing in the world and is idealized by exalting the workers as they have never before been

*Professor Sims visited the U. S. S. R. this past summer, as a member of the American Social Science Committee, who were sent to investigate conditions.

honored. The organized toilers are the new aristocracy who have stepped into the place of the old nobility. The most desirable type of citizen is clearly he who in some capacity contributes by earnest toil to the upbuilding of the Soviet order. The genuineness of this attitude is not to be gainsaid; it is of the very essence of Leninism. Among the youth the slogan is, "Prepare for labor, share in labor," and this they are eagerly doing. To "prepare for labor" is indeed the burden of all education in Russia today, a conception wholly at variance with the American educational scheme, the aim of which is to assist its students to escape exacting toil, or prepare them for professions furnishing ample leisure. I made many inquiries of young men and women, this summer, as to whom they considered the most eligible for marriage. They invariably declared in favor of the working man or woman. So I came out of Russia with the distinct feeling that the dictatorship of the proletariat had at least erected a new ideal of citizenship in making labor peculiarly honorable.

Another thing that does not elude even the superficial globe-trotter on a visit to the Soviet Union is the cordial appreciation and practice of equality. Evidences of this are many and concrete. The old race discriminations of Tsaristic Russia are gone. Doubtless they still live underneath, but the new Russian quickly grinds them under his heel whenever they venture to appear. The elevation of women to the same plane with men is obvious. They enjoy equal privileges and prerogatives, not only in theory but also in practice whether it be in work or in matters of sex. Women are found side by side with men in all industries and in positions of authority. One effect of this had been to cause sex to be taken as a matter of course as perhaps nowhere else in the civilized world.

Classes, in the sense of groupings on the basis of important economic differences, have been eliminated; and the Soviet drive is toward a society that will afford no ground whatsoever for classes of any kind. This, of course, cannot be fully attained until the psychology of the old generation is supplanted by that of a new one. As it is, the term "class" is not being used. The word "category" has been substituted, so that one travels first, second or third category as the case may be, instead of first, second or third class.

This equalitarian attitude is seen in dress. It is also heard in address, for the highest greet the humblest and the humblest the highest as "Tovarish" or "Comrade." The official is not some one set over and above his fellows, but is merely a comrade assigned to his particular work by the group. The people in a peculiar way remain the boss and retain the sense of authority and power. I noticed this in the relation of individuals to the police who are regarded merely as workers delegated to keep order. It is by no means uncommon to hear citizens lecturing policemen to their face about their shortcomings. For instance, our chauffeur on one occasion, after narrowly escaping a crash at a busy intersection, drove up to the curb, called to the traffic officer stationed there, "Come here, Tovarish," and then proceeded to lay him out for failing to regulate the traffic.

Strange to say, the policeman stood, looked, listened, and finally apologized. Imagine the like of it in America! I felt it would be worth a revolution any day to be able to talk to the cops of our American cities that way!

One easily senses a new attitude among the Russians toward the past and the future. I was impressed on many occasions by their effort to break completely with yesterday's ten thousand years. The traditional is definitely repudiated, often with bitter hatred, both in principle and in practice. This appears, for instance, in the abolition of all pre-revolutionary law and legal precedent. In their stead the "revolutionary conscience," regulated by a few fundamental rules of action, is the only guide in courts of justice. Moreover, the result seems to be most wholesome. What country is there that would not profit from a similar repudiation of its legal past!

Naturally, along some lines the effort to shut out the past appears ridiculous; this has been notably true in the fields of literature and music. Fortunately the Soviets have recanted and are now restoring the ancient masterpieces to a more favorable place in their cultural program.

Judging by this rejection of the traditional, you may easily jump to the conclusion that things in Russia are determined by theory, by the Marxian dialectic if you like, and hence are wholly doctrinaire. This, however, is not the case. Nothing is hallowed either by tradition or by theory. You soon become aware of the fact that everything is determined by experimentation, that all theory, even the Marxian ideology, has to be tried out in practice and evaluated by the consequences. Thus the Soviet mind is pragmatic and opportunistic, not doctrinaire and absolutistic.

For the same reason that has caused them to turn their backs upon the past, the new Russians are looking hopefully to the future. So much so, in fact, that the miseries, sacrifices and difficulties of the present are spurned as the nation goes full steam ahead for the millenium which it glimpses "just around the corner"—as our politicians in America say.

Above all the youth of Russia are responding to new motives. One encounters these motives in effective operation in the lives of the new generation that has grown up since the war. The absence of the economic or profit-making and fortune-seeking ambition, so dominant in America, is conspicuous. Private fortunes are, of course, out of the question, and opportunities for profit-making almost non-existent in the Soviet Union. Nevertheless the youth are just as ambitious and have just as much incentive to effort, insofar as I can see, as do youth in the lands believing it is only money that makes the mare go. Russian youth are motivated by the desire to win recognition for service in the building of a new social order. They are challenged by the need for skilled workers, technicians, engineers, leaders, inventors, organizers, professionally trained men and women; and they are responding to that challenge for the glory of doing something useful and having a share in the making of a new world.

For the moment at least, the great adventure of building a socialistic commonwealth has very much the appeal of a call to arms. A war of conquest, over power-ful enemies and stubborn forces, is indeed being waged. The psychology and language of battle is there. All the glamour of a holy crusade attends the struggle. The difference is that the glory of grandiose social reconstruc-tion has been substituted for the heroism of the battle-field. So the youth of the Soviet Union march val-iantly under a new blood-red banner, with the song ever upon their lips:

> "Arise, ye prisoners of starvation!
> Arise, ye wretched of the earth!
> For justice thunders condemnation;
> A better world's in birth."

I think it rather astonishes the visitor to the cities and villages of this land to find so much enthusiasm be-hind such unusual, and as it were, abstract motives. The Westerner, with his age-old background and habits of thought, will naturally question whether it can last. He will be disposed to say, "It is too good to go on." But in my opinion, it is a far sounder judgment to say that we wise men of the West are no wiser than our own experiences and prejudices. There may be wiser men than we in the East. Who knows that a truer and better world is not actually in birth in Muscovy?

Finally, I sensed the passing of Russia's ancient pas-sivity, fatalism, mysticism and helplessness as I mingled with the men and women in scores of places. The old "nicheva" or what-does-it-matter complacency is giv-ing way to a daring assertiveness. The will to achieve coupled with a youthful exuberance has arisen in the drab towns and on the desolate steppes. The old Rus-sian soul full of superstition, servility, senescence and darkness is dying, and a new soul, compound of skepti-cism, boldness, virility and light, is coming to birth. It is as if an aged man should become adolescent again.

I saw the old Russia one Sunday morning at an Or-thodox Greek Cathedral at Rostov on the Don. There a throng of worshippers stood at mass, bowed down crying, "Lord, have mercy," kissed the ikons in abject obeisance, drank holy water and were anointed by the priest. Among them a score of beggars plied their trade and without the Cathedral door hundreds asked alms. In the plaza before the building a bazaar was being held where wares were noisily vended. It was a mediaeval scene, a mediaeval atmosphere, a mediaeval people and a mediaeval mind. It was old Russia, the Russia of a thousand years, the Russia that is dead and will soon be no more.

I walked a few blocks away from this place to a beautiful park of culture and rest, as it is called in Rus-sia, where a far greater number of people had resorted. There I saw and heard a marvelous new thing. It was a full symphonic orchestra playing a classical program, the opening number of which was Schubert's *Unfinished Symphony*. That orchestra was led by a little nine-year-old girl, a musical prodigy, far-famed in all south-ern Russia. As I listened and wondered at what I saw, the thought occurred to me that this little child in the role of musical director was symbolic of the soul of the new Russia, the living, growing, aspiring, achieving un-believable Russia, Russia that once was old but now is young again.

Christmas Eve, 1929

The stars hung down so close—like candles set
In great dark windows on this holy night;
I saw above me the familiar fret
Of constellations, threading still their bright
And silent paths across the firmament
After so long a stretch of human years.
And as I watched, like a rich sacrament,
Christmas descended. The dim press of tears
And laughter crowded round my heart again,
The echo of old carols sung at dawn
In the low hills, and here upon the plain;
The happy sight of faces that are gone;
And thought of multitudes I shall not see
Carolling through the Christmas-tides to be!
—Katharine Shepard Hayden '18·

A Trip to Oberlin-in-Shansi

BY PROFESSOR WALTER M. HORTON*

WE had been looking forward to our trip to Shansi ever since January 6th, when we were formally entrusted, in Finney Chapel, with an illuminated leather-bound letter, bearing the greetings of Oberlin-in-America to Oberlin-in-Shansi. We had been hoping that neither war nor bandits would prevent our delivering it. Well, we found that travel conditions in North China were better than they had been for years. Common opposition to Japan had put an end, temporarily, to civil war; and there was even talk of turning the boycott against any party leaders who renewed it. The railways used to be seized periodically by soldiers, who lolled in the first and second class compartments while the general public had to ride in flat-cars or walk. This year the trains were running with reasonable speed—although no one knew precisely when they were supposed to start and arrive—and they were kept fairly clean. As for bandits and train robbers, their attacks were not numerous, comparatively polite, and at any rate unpredictable. A train was robbed on the main line, between Tehchow and Tientsin, just the night before I came through; but the robbers delayed the train only an hour, and as no one resisted, no one was hurt.

We had expected to enter North China by rail from Shanghai, *via* Nanking and Tientsin; but as the Shanghai-Nanking line was torn up during the war and hostile armies were still facing each other at "the front" twenty miles out of the city, while the peace parleys seemed to drag on from one deadlock to another, we decided to avoid the war area, and, lingering in Shanghai just long enough to meet Dr. K'ung, proceeded to Tientsin by boat.

Our first impressions of North China were rather unprepossessing. Our queer little boat, the *Tungchow*—which, by the way, was captured by pirates a few years ago and taken off with all her passengers and crew to the pirate islands below Canton—had the misfortune to miss the morning tide at Taku Bar, at the mouth of the Pei Ho; and there we stayed all day, while the fishermen sailed forth, made their day's haul, and returned. At last, late in the afternoon, there was water enough to float us over the bar and take us a few miles up the muddy little river to Tangku, the port of Tientsin. And what a scene on the wharf at Tangku!—a ragged, frenzied mob of starving coolies, fighting each other for the privilege of clambering aboard first, to handle our freight and baggage; jumping for the rope ladders at the risk of tumbling into the water, and swarming up the sides like a boarding-party of Captain Kidd's; while a man with a long bamboo pole vainly tried to keep order among them by cracking them vigorously on the skull and knocking them senseless beneath the feet of their competitors. No one was killed, and the under-dogs emerged grinning resignedly; but I never saw the brute struggle for existence more dramatically displayed by human beings.

At midnight that same day we arrived at Peking (now officially but not popularly known as Peiping). where we were met by Stephen Pyle, (Seminary '12-'15) of the Union Church and my old friend Timothy Lew of Yenching University. We motored through the broad, dark streets of the Imperial City, getting a glimpse of the lakes that surround the Winter Palace, glistening in the star-light; halted at the north-west gate while the guard demanded our credentials and pushed open the ponderous wooden door; and then bumped for an hour over a dark, rutty road, guarded by armed soldiers, until we reached the campus of Yenching University at one-thirty in the morning. Two weeks later, after a delightful time at Yenching, a trip to the Great Wall, and a trip to Shantung province, where I attended the American Board meetings at Tenchow and lectured at Cheeloo University in Tsinan—meeting many Oberlin graduates and friends in both places—we were at last ready for our long trip inland to Shansi.

Phil Dutton and Albert Hansske of the American Board Mission in Taiku had arranged to accompany us

*This article is the second of a series of three by Professor Horton, concerning the three main stages in the Hortons' recent trip around the world.

Professor Horton Escorted to *the Boys' School, Shansi, by Dean Ch 'iao*

all the way from Peking, as they were just on their way back from the Tenchow meetings. Thanks to their knowledge of Chinese, we had no difficulties whatsoever. After a comfortable over-night trip from Peking to Shih-Chia-Chwang on the Hankow line, we had just time to breakfast at the French hotel before taking the narrow-gauge train on the line built by the French some years ago between Shih-Chia-Chwang and Taiyuanfu, the capital of Shansi province. It is a splendid piece of engineering and in excellent condition, since its narrow gauge has made it impossible for any war-lord to appropriate its rolling-stock for use in distant places. The four of us had lunch served in our compartment, and I never had a better meal.

The trip was beautiful. After a short run across a plain checkered by wheat and millet patches and dotted with groups of tall grave-stones—quite different from the semi-circular graves which pock-mark the hills in the south—we reached the Mother and Son Pass, the gateway to Shansi, guarded by ancient watch-towers and quite recently by machine-gun nests. Thence we wound our way for over a hundred miles up a river valley, where a scanty stream of water was utilized to the full in irrigation ditches and in scores of tiny flour mills with thatched roofs and over-shot wheels, turning sidewise. The bare mountains were terraced high up their sides, and green things were growing in the rich wind-blown soil wherever a supply of water could be led or carried. Up nearer the divide at the top of the valley we passed lime-kilns, coal mines and iron mines, showing that this is potentially the richest industrial area in China—especially since it is sheltered from military attack by distance from the sea-coast and high mountain barriers. For several miles we passed along the rim of a deep canyon, with a pretty village built on the opposite edge, and waterfalls springing from the rocky sides of the abyss. Finally we crossed the divide, descended another valley on the other side, and came out into the broad high plateau where Taiku is located.

Sam Wilson and Dean Ch'iao were at the station (Yutze) to meet us and we had plenty of talk and laughter as we drove the twenty miles that separated us from the school. At last a great ridge of mountains loomed above the horizon, with a porcelain pagoda on one peak and Feng-Shan, an ancient monastery, on another; and a moment later we could pick out Hemingway Dormitory and other school buildings, lying on the plain about four miles from the foot of the mountains. As we approached the walls of the compound, we found both sides of the road lined with students, teachers and Taiku missionaries; and as we got out of the car to return their

One of the Moon-Gates in the Flower Garden

greetings we found ourselves marching behind a squad of students playing strange fife-like music on Chinese reed instruments, while strings of fire-crackers popped in our honor, and Roger Hawkins led the crowd in an Oberlin College yell. Movie cameras whirred and clicked as we shook hands right and left; and I was obliged to mount the wall, in a very unkempt and un-shaven condition—toilet rooms on even the best trains in China are too dirty for much use—and say a few words in response. I ended by saying "Thank you" in my best Chinese, whereat the students burst into shouts of laughter. Then we were led in through rock-gardens, arching bridges, court-yards and moon-gates, past the graves of the Boxer martyrs, into the residence compound, where the Wilsons made us welcome.

We were in Taiku eight days and busy every moment. I should hate to estimate how many speeches I made, or how many groups of people I met. In all these matters I was nobly reinforced by my wife, who blossomed out into a most effective public speaker, and was, I suspect, more popular with the students than I was. Her lively manner and clear enunciation made her speeches easy to understand (for those who had any English) even before they were interpreted, whereas my long, complex sentences must have strained their attention and taxed the powers of the interpreters. The most memorable occasion, of course, was the meeting at which the Oberlin letter was formally delivered. It was held in the evening in an open court-yard hung with Chinese lanterns and flags of all nations, filled to overflowing with teachers and students, while the speakers stood on the "theatre-stage" of an old temple now used as a sort of school museum. There was more reedy music by the school orchestra; English songs by groups of girl students; speeches by Dean Ch'iao and by the two visitors; and finally, two plays, accompanied by a professional Chinese orchestra from Taiku City. The first was a play in classical style with much quavery music and monologue, having to do with a quack doctor who contracts with a mother to brew a potion which will cure her son of his ambition to be an actor; the other was a burlesque of a Japanese invasion, in which the foe was finally rolled upon the floor by a combination of Chinese boxing and ancient Chinese sword-play. One expected at any moment to see some one's head roll upon the floor; but they always ducked just in time. Just before our departure another ceremony was arranged, at which we were given a reply letter, bound in boards, with Chinese lettering in gold. (This was not considered sufficiently ornate, so another letter was later prepared and sent in its stead.)

The whole community, needless to say, was most hospitable to us, the North (school) compound and the South (missionary) compound vying with one another in dining and tea-ing us and showing us their work. We were very favorably impressed with the work of the Oberlin representatives in their English classes. They are under the instruction and supervision of a permanent teacher, Miss Munger, who also does much volunteer work with self-help, social service and religious educational groups. Ray Moyer's agricultural and industrial work is splendid; though still in the experimental stage, it seems likely to become the backbone of the curriculum in the near future, and may make our school a center from which the agricultural and industrial development of the whole province will be influenced. My wife was particularly impressed with Miss Wu's work in home economics, and Miss Liu's work in physical education in the Girls' School. It was hard to believe that the hardy-looking girls romping about the playground had been hollow-chested and unable to run without staggering barely six months ago.

Perhaps the most memorable day of our stay in Shansi was the day when we packed our belongings into two two-wheeled carts (covered wagon style) and, partly riding and partly walking, set out with Sam Wilson for the mountains. It was after eleven when we reached the foot of the trail which leads to Feng-Shan, and we were already hot and tired, so we stopped at a little shrine for a short rest, and abandoning the idea of climbing to the top, ate our lunch at a beautiful temple partway up the side, where several members of the missionary group overtook us. We filled our cups at a little spring in a deep, cool grotto in the mountain-side, where a lovely little goddess, covered with gold-leaf, sat cross-legged upon a rock in the middle of the pool. My wife was so intent upon viewing the goddess that she nearly fell into the pool in the semi-darkness. Afterwards we went through the temples, and were interested to see that the main sanctuary with its three great Buddhas sitting in calm, disdainful detachment, was apparently neglected by the people, while certain little side-chapels where one sets up an image of a man-child in hope of getting one, were full of votive offerings. On a high point of rock near by was a pole hung with sheets of iron or tin which are dipped in water and hung up in the wind on the mountain-side, as a sure means of producing rain. As we stood on this point, we could look far off across the plain, and counted six separate dust-storms whirling along in different directions, in the shape of miniature cyclones. (One of them caught us at dinner on the porch next day and drove us indoors in a hurry). As I had a lecture to deliver at 4:30 I borrowed a bicycle, and pedalled back along precarious footpaths to Taiku, in the wake of Ray Moyer and Dr. Hemingway. We stopped on the way to climb up the steps of another temple in the foot-hills and to look at some deposits of neolithic pottery in an ancient water-course; so, with the additional delay of one or two "spills" at sharp corners (I haven't ridden a bicycle for twenty years!) I got back, dusty and decidedly lame and bedraggled, just when I was due to lecture. What I said in the lecture or how brilliant my conversation was at the Oberlin alumni dinner that night, I shouldn't dare say; but I know I had a great day!

On May eighteenth, just a week before we were due to leave China, we set out again for Peking from Taiku, laden with gifts (including a huge straw case in which to carry them) and accompanied by Dean Ch'iao, who kindly volunteered to see us safely back. It was well that he came with us, for when we got to Shih-Chia-Chwang we found that the express train to Peking did not run at all that night. We had to pass the night in the hotel—which proved cleaner than we feared—and take a slow train next day, which got to "S. C. C." at 4 a. m. and Peking at 3 p. m. Breakfast proved such a farce that we ate an orange for lunch and let it go at that. We had ordered poached eggs, toast and tea. The tea came first and was made of water so full of sediment that it might have come from the Yangtze River. We had to teach the cook how to toast the bread. The eggs were delivered to us floating in turbid water two inches deep in a soup plate. So when we finally met our friends the Hungs at the Wagon-Lits Hotel—having missed a luncheon appointment with them there—we felt decidedly travel-worn. But what fun would there be in world touring if one had no mishaps to write home about!

One episode on this tedious trip back to Peking was worth all the discomforts we had to endure: a long conversation with Sam Deane of the Peking School of Engineering Practice, who got on the train at Pao-ting-fu and spent several hours talking with us in our compartment. Mr. Deane is an exceptionally well-informed man, who travels extensively throughout China, supervising engineering projects undertaken by his pupils; and his opinion on industrial and educational developments in China carries much weight. It was therefore most impressive to us when he declared that, in his sober judgment, Oberlin-in-Shansi was *the most significant Middle School in China.* He reasoned thus: (1) Shansi province is the key to the future development of China, agriculturally, industrially and in every other way, since it is the one province sufficiently removed from the areas of civil disturbance and foreign interference to carry on uninterrupted progress, and since it is exceptionally rich in coal and iron. (2) Oberlin-in-Shansi is already counted as the best school in Shansi province, in recognition of which government officials in Taiyuanfu sometimes send their children to Taiku, instead of educating them in the capital. (3) If, instead of trying to become a University, competing with Yenching and Cheeloo—a plan already abandoned—our school is content to remain a Middle School, giving special attention to agricultural and industrial education along lines already suggested by Ray Moyer, then it may become *the key to the development of Shansi, as Shansi is the key to the development of China.* The intense interest in the school shown by the people of the province this spring, when our three-day annual fair and exhibit was visited by *over ten thousand people each day,* including many government officials, foreshadows the great possibilities that may be realized when our new agricultural-industrial program is more fully developed.

This estimate of the potential significance of Oberlin-in-Shansi was substantially confirmed during our last week in Peking, when we met with a large group of Oberlin alumni under the leadership of Mr. Fei of the Peking Craft Shop—who treated us like a parent, and personally introduced us to the wonders of the Forbidden City—and when we talked with many of the leaders of the missionary and educational groups in the old capital. Not all agreed with Mr. Deane's whole argument: Mr. Fei, for example, suggested that Shansi province was almost *too* isolated to help the development of the rest of China; but all agreed upon the wisdom of the plan to use our school as a sort of John-Frederick-Oberlin center, which may do for Shansi province what the good John Frederick did for his parish in the Vosges—improving its roads and crops and industries as a firm basis for the growth of its moral and intellectual life. So we emerged from North China with the settled conviction that, in spite of student strikes and faculty friction and financial difficulties, Oberlin-in-Shansi is a great school, with a future even greater than her past, and that she deserves the whole-hearted coöperation of her sister school in America, and of every Oberlin alumnus.

'32 Meets the Realities of the "Depression"

BY IVANORE V. BARNES '18
Secretary of the Bureau of Appointments

THE Bureau of Appointments during the past six weeks has been in correspondence with the majority of the members of the Class of 1932 in connection with securing information for the directory published in the last issue of the Magazine. We have also been making a study of the occupational distribution of this youngest group of alumni. We were glad to learn that at least sixty-three men and women had full-time positions, that ten had temporary work, and that one hundred and four were able to go on with graduate study and vocational ·training. A very large proportion of those engaged in graduate study have been successful in securing scholarships. However, many of the responses to our letters and the size of the group of men and women not yet located in positions reveal a startling and disheartening situation, particularly when one considers the individuals involved—their financial problems, the let-down that comes from suddenly being at loose ends in contrast to the various activities of college, the disappointment on the part of those who have prepared themselves professionally for teaching and who have made every effort to secure positions. Between ninety and one hundred and twenty of the members of last year's graduating class have not yet been able to secure positions. Many of this number are in debt for part of their college expenses; most of them are willing to do almost any sort of work as a "pot-boiler" until there are opportunities in the fields of their chief occupational interests. Sixty-nine of the one hundred and twenty have professional training for teaching the various high school subjects, special subjects, and instrumental music. Following is the actual statistical tabulation:

OCCUPATIONAL DISTRIBUTION OF THE CLASS OF

1932

Note: This tabulation includes students who completed their courses between September 1, 1931 and October 15, 1932. Figures enclosed in parentheses are duplicates and are not included in totals. They indicate that the type of work is also involved in the main occupations of the graduate.

BUSINESS	Men	Women	Total
Insurance—Office Work	1		1
Underwriting	1		1
Investments	1		1
Manufacturing—In Training	2		2
Office Work	2		2
Secretarial		1	1
Selling	2	3	5
Merchandising—In Training	1		1

EDUCATION	Men	Women	Total
Teaching			
College—Instructing	2	3	5
Graduate Assisting	1	(3) 1	(3)
Public Schools			
High Schools			
Junior		1	1
Junior and Senior	1	4	5
Unspecified		1	1
Grammar School		4	4
Supervising Special Subjects			
Music	1	5	6
Physical Education		2	2
Private Schools		3	3
Foreign Mission School	1	1	2
Institution		1	1
School of Nursing		1	1
Private Lessons	1	5	6
Unspecified		1	1

	Men	Women	Total
JOURNALISM—Newspaper	1	2	3
MUSIC	2		2

SOCIAL WORK	Men	Women	Total
Child Welfare		(1)	(1)
Family Welfare		4 (1)	4 (1)
Group Service	1		1
Institutional Service		(2)	(2)
TEMPORARILY EMPLOYED	4	6	10
Total doing Remunerative work	25	48 (7)	73 (7)

	Men	Women	Total
AT HOME		4	4
TRAVEL	1	2	3
INDETERMINATE	10	8	18
NOT YET LOCATED IN POSITIONS	29	62	91

MADONNA OF THE VEIL
(Copy of the lost Raphael madonna, owned by the Allen Art Museum)

In numbers, and but these few,
I sing thy birth, O Jesu,
Thou pretty baby, born here,
With superabundant scorn here,
Who for thy princely port here,
    Hadst for thy place
    Of birth, a base
Out-stable for thy court here.

Instead of neat enclosures
Of interwoven osiers,
Instead of fragrant posies
Of daffodils and roses,
Thy cradle, kingly stranger,
    As gospel tells,
    Was nothing else
But here a homely manger.

Robert Herrick (1591-1674).

GRADUATE STUDY AND VOCATIONAL TRAINING

	Men	Women	Total
Aeronautical Engineering	1		1
Botany	2	1	3
Business Administration	7	2	9
Chemistry	1		1
Classics	1		1
Dentistry	1		1
Economics	3		3
Education	2		2
English	5	1	6
Eurythmics		1	1
Fine Arts	1	4	5
French	1	1	2
Geology	1		1
German	1	1	2
History	3		3
International Studies		1	1
Kindergarten Training		1	1
Law	4		4
Library Science	1	3	4
Mathematics	2		2
Medicine	10	1	11
Music	3	5	8
Nursing		1	1
Physical Education	2	2	4
Physics	1		1
Political Science	2	2	4
Religious Education		3	3
Secretarial Training		5	5
Sociology	1	6	7
Theology	3		3
Zoology	2	2	4
	61	43	104
Total	126	167	293

It is small comfort to those who are eager for work and to those who are interested in the progress of these young alumni to be told, "But Oberlin's recent grad-nates are no worse off than the classes going out from all of the colleges; in fact, a larger proportion of them are either placed or in graduate study than is the case in a number of colleges." Such comments may give the young graduate the assurance that no personal stigma is attached to his being without work; just as frequently they give him an overwhelming sense of the competition in which he may be submerged if he does have an opportunity to apply for an actual position. Perhaps it is well that he should see the reality of competition in order that he may have some comprehension of how important it is to make use of his best qualities and of his most influential references when he is applying for a position. Even with an imposing array of qualifications and of influential references as well as with a positively favorable impression made upon the employer, the candidate just out of college frequently loses the position because the employer decides in favor of an experienced candidate whose desperate need for work makes him willing to accept a position and a salary gauged for a beginner, according to present standards—a salary far below what a beginner would have been paid four years ago. Occasionally the young graduate's application is discarded in favor of someone who, though he may not be nearly so well qualified for the given position, is well known in the community and who is appointed to the position out of consideration for a personal or a family loss in position or in income. While one may sympathize with the employer in his quandary over choosing between a professionally trained candidate just out of college—one who needs to earn his living—and a more mature applicant whose professional qualifications for the specific position are inferior, but who has a more obvious financial problem to meet—one's sober judgment is inclined toward regarding the filling of a position with the person *best fitted to do the work* as the policy that will have the best social and economic results in the long run. It is true that many able people of excellent experience are out of work through no fault of their own and that many of them need work desperately. It is none the less true that there are some young graduates of extraordinary promise, fresh from professional training or with a background that would enable them to work into various types of positions, whose ability and whose need for work merit their receiving equally serious consideration along with the more mature applicants for positions.

The whole employment situation is at present tremendously involved and complicated. The employers in business firms, organizations and school systems have no simple task, and the human factors in any given situation are often baffling, particularly if they constitute the basis for an important decision. Certainly, one cannot blame a mature person who needs work for marshalling all of his powers to succeed in the competition for a position. In the majority of cases, it may be true that experienced candidates merit first consideration for the all too few opportunities for remunerative employment. Nevertheless, there are instances in which a more serious consideration of the young applicant just out of college would not be unfair to more experienced candidates and in which the firm or organization would find it to its interest to employ the younger graduate.

We note with pleasure the numerous instances of good sportsmanship and the many wholesome examples of making the best of a bad situation on the part of "the unemployed" of the Class of 1932. Many of them are doing volunteer work that has some bearing upon their chief occupational interests. Some of them are working temporarily at jobs paying ten or twelve dollars a week, and they speak of "being lucky to have at least something." They refer to themselves humorously in such terms as:

"Just another college graduate without a job"

"Another member of the great army of the unemployed"

"One more victim of the depression"

"Personally, the depression is the same huge success"

Next week, we register the members of the Class of 1933. We hope that any of our alumni who learn of vacancies, or prospective vacancies, into which recent graduates might fit will bear in mind the fact that about a hundred or more of last year's graduates and close to two hundred of the present seniors will be available for work.

EDITORIAL

(Continued from page 69)

universities to relate their facts to living, or a desperate blindness on the part of politicians to the fact that facts transcend polities. This discrepancy still holds good, but there are a few signs, a very few, that the long famine is drawing to a close, and that a practical step towards a more rational way of government may yet be taken.

Men and Women of Oberlin's Hundred Years

Asa Mahan, *first president of Oberlin College, reached Oberlin in May, 1835. Eastern by birth, he had been a minister in Cincinnati and a Trustee of Lane Seminary; had sympathized with the Lane Rebels in their anti-slavery stand, and had been "discovered" by Father Shipherd in the course of his roundabout journey to New York. Mahan was then thirty-six years of age.*

President Mahan was a highly positive man, a radical and aggressive leader. He hesitated at nothing needful to the welfare of the College, even manual labor. It was President Mahan who brought to Oberlin the admirable practice of hearing both sides of a question. Any doctrine could be expounded, but it had to be answered; and so effective were both Mr. Mahan and Mr. Finney as debaters that many of the fanciful theories abounding in that day took no hold in the hot-bed of Oberlin.

While President Mahan's administration was both creditable and successful, his positiveness exposed him to difficulties. It led him at one time into a crusade against the "heathen classics," into a warm espousal of the special doctrine of sanctification, and into a certain measure of antagonism with some of his colleagues. In 1850 he was invited to the presidency of a new college in Cleveland; went later to Adrian College, and died in England in 1892.

Charles Grandison Finney, *(see outside cover), perhaps the greatest single name in Oberlin's history, arrived a month after President Mahan. It was Finney, the greatest evangelist of his time, that really opened the College doors to the colored: such action was his stipulation to the Trustees as the condition of his coming. Once at Oberlin, Finney remained until his death in 1875, having served as teacher since 1835, as president from 1851 to 1865, as pastor until 1872.*

It is hard to take the measure of a man like Finney. He and his thought were the product of no "seminary" or "school." Until the time of his conversion his training had been legal, and afterwards his chief theological guides were the Bible and his own powerful mind. That mind was extraordinary in its range and grasp, the personality of the man magnetic, his emotional capacity deep. It is wrong to think of him as cold and formalistic; on the contrary, his capacity for feeling was excessive, but it was poured out in one channel, tempered keen as a sword, by the quality of his intellect.

President Finney was an evangelist, not an educator. His mission in life was to save souls, and he valued Oberlin chiefly as a place where young souls might be saved, and where men might be trained to save other souls. The College must be thankful to him, both for his labors and for the gift of his great name.

John Morgan *was no such conscious king among men as Finney, but he was one of the best loved teachers Oberlin has ever had. Irish by birth, a graduate of Williams College, he came in 1835 as Professor of New Testament Literature and Exegesis. He was the dear friend and co-pastor of President Finney, and the companion and friend of President Fairchild. His term of service extended over forty-seven fruitful years.*

Morgan was a man of learning, broad culture and gentle heart. There was said to be no study in the curriculum in which he could not give instruction at an hour's warning, as successfully as if it were his own specialty. His breadth and sanity of view was especially valuable in the early days, when the cause of education seemed for a time likely to lose its rightful place in the interests of theology.

"His teaching," says President Fairchild, "was on a broad and generous plan, dealing with essential facts, touching the nature of things. . . . (As a preacher) he felt it necessary to present the truth systematically, even at the sacrifice of immediate impressive force." Many remember his beautiful reading of hymns.

Professor Morgan wrote little, spending his force in living and teaching. He died in 1884 at the age of 82.

John Oscar Lofberg

BY PROFESSOR LOUIS E. LORD '97

John Oscar Lofberg was born at Jacobstad, Finland, April 21, 1882. He died at Oberlin November 10, 1932. He was a graduate of the John B. Stetson University, De Land, Florida, in 1905 and of the University of Chicago the same year. He received his Doctorate from the University of Chicago in 1914. His teaching experience was unusually wide and varied. He taught at Stetson University; he was principal of the Sleepy Eye High School in Minnesota; instructor in Classics at Bradley Polytechnic Institute, Peoria, Illinois; assistant in Greek at the University of Chicago; instructor in Latin at the Oak Park High School; assistant professor of Greek at the University of Texas; associate professor of Classics at Queen's University, Kingston, Canada; professor of Classics and head of the department at Washington and Lee University, Lexington, Virginia. The unusual compliment was paid him of giving him an appointment at the summer quarter at the University of Chicago in two successive years. Last summer he taught at the University of North Carolina. He came to Oberlin College as professor of Classics in 1927.

His activities outside of the work at Oberlin were notable. He was for two years president of the Classical Club of Greater Cleveland; he had been secretary-treasurer of the Ohio Classical Conference and secretary-treasurer of the Classical Association of the Middle West and South; last spring he resigned this latter office to accept the editorship of *The Classical Journal*, the organ of this association. This is the most widely circulated classical journal in the world. Although his editorship had extended only over two issues, his personality was already being felt in its columns and he was laying the foundations of what his friends expected to be a wide reputation as a classical editor. He was associated with Professor R. J. Bonner of the University of Chicago in the publication of a Greek Reader. This is now in press. His articles on philological subjects and on the pedagogical phases of the teaching of Classics are well known. He had made his mark in the classical world as an administrator, as a scholar and as a teacher.

He had been at Oberlin for only five years, yet he seemed already a large and integral part of the College and community. Few men have in so short a space commanded such respect or won such love.

Among teachers of the Classics he was recognized as a finished scholar. An authority on Athenian legal practice, he still found time to write on other matters. There was about his scholarship a

certain quality which, for lack of a better term, might be called ripeness; the quality which enables a student after mastering the minutiae of a subject to cast aside the irrelevant details and survey his field with a breadth of vision that only wide reading and seasoned judgment can give. His place among the scholars of America was secure and promotion to a place in one of the great universities awaited him.

"He seemed to me one of the finest and most admirable of men; and the loss is an extremely heavy one for all of us. Please accept my most cordial sympathy, both for yourself and your department and Oberlin College."

I take this almost at random from a pile of letters that lie before me from classical teachers in secondary schools and almost every college in the country. Nor are these letters merely conventional expressions of sympathy. Through them all runs a note of personal bereavement that shows how vital were the ties of friendship which he had made. Many recall the buoyancy of his spirit, his ready wit, his mellow humor, his kindness and eagerness to help (in one of the places where he taught they remembered his care for the old ladies of the community), his varied interests, his love of nature and of art, of plants and flowers, of pictures and music, of the drama and of literature. Yet the one quality which all who knew him emphasize, the basis on which all this esteem for him rested, was his unusual capacity for friendship, that largeness of heart, those generous impulses that made him beloved wherever he was known. His passing leaves the world for his friends an emptier place; they long in vain for that

"Paulum quid libet allocutionis,
Maestius lacrimis Simonideis."

Rawdon Elected President of N. E. O. T. A.

Howard L. Rawdon '04, for the past twenty-five years superintendent of schools in Oberlin, was elected president of the Northeastern Ohio Teachers' Association at its annual meeting in Cleveland October 28. He had served as vice-president of the Association last year, and has been a member of the executive committee for three years and a member of the Association for thirty.

He presided at the Oberlin Alumni luncheon in Hotel Carter, at which Professor Robert S. Fletcher '20 reviewed his studies in the early history of Oberlin.

Benjamin F. Stanton of Alliance, Oberlin '96, was re-elected executive secretary of the N. E. O. T. A. for the coming year.

Wheat for the Hungry

Alumni who have followed with interest the development of the Wheat Plan and Three-Cent Meal originated by Dr. Robert E. Brown '01 of the Graduate School of Theology last fall, from its beginnings to the final passage of the Capper Bill authorizing the distribution of Government wheat to the needy through the Red Cross, will be further interested in these excerpts from the *Red Cross Courier* for September, 1932:

"The following summary report of wheat distribution at the close of business on July 30 will be found as illuminating as it is informing of the immensity of this relief operation, now to be continued until 95,000,000 bushels of wheat will have been delivered to relieve 'the needs of human consumption':

Chapters applying for flour—3,113.

Chapters applying for stock feed—332.

Families to be aided by the flour—3,188,290.

Families to be aided by the stock feed—179,038.

Barrels of flour requisitioned—3,254,359.

Tons of feed requisitioned—223,921.

Bushels of wheat committed—35,312,028.

"Flour has been shipped into every county but one in six New England States. Chapters in nine states, as follows, had requisitioned flour for every county: Maine, New Hampshire, Vermont, Massachusetts, Connecticut, Delaware, South Carolina, Utah and Michigan. Rhode Island, South Dakota and Washington Chapters had obtained flour for every county but one in each state. States which have received flour for all but two counties are West Virginia, Indiana, Oklahoma, New Mexico, Arizona, Nevada, California and Idaho; all but three counties, Ohio and Wisconsin; and all but four counties, New Jersey, Florida and Tennessee. Illinois has requisitioned flour for all but six counties, Pennsylvania for all but eleven counties, and New York for all but thirteen counties, including the counties of Greater New York. Kansas shows fewer counties asking for flour than any state.

"An average of three weeks has been required for flour delivery from the 'order receiving desk' at National Headquarters to the railroad siding at destination. Milling and transportation authorities agree that this is rapid and efficient handling of business."

This and further information concerning the actual workings of the plan will be found in an article called "The Nation's Wheat for the Nation's Hungry," written by Dr. Brown for *The Congregationalist* of October 20. As stated above, the Red Cross expects to continue wheat relief throughout the present winter.

Trustees Vote $80,000 Cut

In view of decreased income from College endowment funds, the Board of Trustees in its annual meeting November 11 authorized that a saving of $80,000 be made in the budget of the present school year. The Budget Committee of Faculty and Trustees has been given power to discharge this task. In view of an operating deficit of $26,484.34 during 1931-32, as well as continuing shrinkage of income during the present year, such action was felt to be peculiarly necessary. The College has already been functioning on a program of special economy during the last nine or ten months.

As a result of the alumni ballot, Dr. Robert A. Millikan was elected to succeed himself as Alumni Trustee for the term of six years beginning January 1, 1933. Dr. Millikan has been a Trustee continuously since 1918.

According to President Wilkins' Report, submitted to and accepted by the Board, the year 1931-32 witnessed a large falling off in gifts to the College. The total received was $413,302.47, of which $357,524.14 went to capital, $1,-648.11 to Endowment and Building Fund, and $54,130.22 to current use. Among the outstanding benefactions were the $10,000 scholarship endowment for the Conservatory of Music, the gift of Mrs. George Bennett Siddall of the Conservatory Class of 1891; a contribution of $2,000 toward the fund for a new women's gymnasium from Mrs. Lucien C. Warner; two annual prize scholarships in economics, one to be awarded to a junior and one to a senior, the gift of Colonel A. L. Mercer '11; $50,000 from the estate of Mr. S. E. Matter '89, ultimate use by the College unrestricted; $10,000 from the estate of Senator Theodore E. Burton '72 for endowment; and $1,000 from the estate of Dr. William E. Barton of the Theological Class of 1890, toward the endowment of the Graduate School of Theology.

In addition to the some $100,000 annually appearing in the budget for scholarship aid, the Trustees last year appropriated an extra $13,000 for an emergency aid fund, and about $10,000 additional was received in current gifts towards the same purpose. The total amount loaned to students in 1931-32, irrespective of the above, was $43,989.15. It is anticipated that this year the need will be even greater, both for loan funds and for student emergency relief.

Plans for the Physics Building and the new Heating Plant have been completed, but cannot be realized until funds can be found. Plans for the Auditorium are still under active consideration. Chief accessions to College property during the present year have been Noah Hall, new men's dormitory and first unit of the projected Men's Campus, and the property of the Oberlin Kindergarten-Primary Training School, which was transferred to the College July 7.

According to the Treasurer's report, the total assets, including buildings and equipment, amount to $24,515,763.35 as of 1932.

The following leaves of absence were granted: Mr. Reuel B. Frost, Instructor in Geology and Geography, for the second semester of the present year; for 1933-34, Professor Louis D. Hartson the Psychology Department, Professor William E. Utterback of the Department of Public Speaking, Dr. Whitelaw R. Morrison, Professor of Hygiene and Physical Education; for the first semester of 1933-34, Professor R. A. Jelliffe of the Department of English; for the second semester of 1933-34, Professor William D. Cairns of the Mathematics Department, Professor Oscar Jaszi of the Department of Political Science, Professor Harry N. Holmes of the Chemistry Department, and Miss Frances G. Nash, Dean of Conservatory women. Dean Thomas W. Graham of the Graduate School of Theology will be granted leave from December 8, 1933, to May 31, 1934.

The Trustees present were President Ernest H. Wilkins, President of the Board; Dr. Dan F. Bradley of Cleveland, Mr. E. W. Brouse of Akron, Mr. James H. Causey of Rockford, Ill., Mr. Cleaveland R. Cross of Cleveland, Miss Beatrice Doerschuk of Bronxville, N. Y., Mr. Clayton K. Fauver of New York, Dr. Joel B. Hayden of Hudson, Ohio, Mr. A. R. Horr of Cleveland, Mr. Clarence C. Johnson of New York, Mr. C. H. Kirshner of Kansas City, Mo., Mr. Amos B. McNairy of Manchester, Vt., Mr. Amos C. Miller of Chicago, Mr. John L. Severance of Cleveland, Dr. Jay T. Stocking of St. Louis, Mo., Mr. Lucien T. Warner of Bridgeport, Conn., and Mr. B. B. Williams of Mt. Vernon, Ohio.

Centennial Calendar for 1933

On sale at the Secretary's office somewhere around the fifteenth of December, will be the College's 1933 Calendar, centennial in theme. In addition to the twelve black and white photographs of present Oberlin buildings and scenes, will be twenty-seven accompanying pencil sketches in red, made by Miss Margaret Schauffler '18, of the Department of Fine Arts, and representing some of the buildings and men that have formed the visible part of Oberlin's past history.

The supply of calendars available will be limited; the price, as last year, will be forty cents.

Van Cleef Made Trustee

Frank Chapman Van Cleef '04, for the past two years President of the Alumni Association, has accepted the position of Trustee to the College, a post to which he was elected at the annual meeting of the Board on November 11. His election fills the vacancy left by the death of George W. Morgan '97, in March, 1931.

Holding his A.B. from Oberlin, Mr. Van Cleef received his LL.B. from Columbia University in 1907. He was for many years a resident of Akron, moving from there to New York City, where he is now a member of the firm of Investment Counsel, Cox, Van Cleef and Jordan.

Frank C. Van Cleef

That Mr. Van Cleef is eminently qualified for his new duties is evidenced both by his active interest in College affairs and by the responsibilities and leadership he has assumed in the Alumni Association. In addition to the presidency, he was this year made chairman of the Alumni Committee which is to plan for the Centennial Commencement in June; he was a member, several years ago, of the Alumni Committee on "How may a college test its product?"; during the Endowment Campaign of 1923 he served as co-chairman of the Akron district. His son John graduated from Oberlin in 1931.

In addition to his business and alumni activities, Mr. Van Cleef has served as officer and as Trustee in two church organizations, was a member of the Board of Education in Hudson, Ohio, and was for three years Chairman of that Board; has taken notable part in civic and industrial movements, and has been a Member of the Board of Editors of the Columbia Law Review.

America Votes

CHAPEL ADDRESS BY PRESIDENT WILKINS ON NOVEMBER 8

Forty million American citizens will vote today.

Through what different scenes will they converge to the polling booths, in what different ways, from what different homes, or places of work, or haunts of idleness! Down the deep quietness of mountain valleys they come, across continuous plains, by mast-topped wharves, through white and green neat villages, through sprawling brickish towns, through the shouting canyons that are city streets, in sunlight, under cloud, through storm, in stagnant heat, in chilling wind; walking they come—hurriedly, slowly—on horseback, by wagon, by automobile, by bus, by train, by subway, by ferry, by canoe, by plane; from cottages they come, from toppling shacks, from walled estates, from adobe huts, from high soft-rugg'd apartments, and from seething tenements; from corner groceries and from department stores, from fields and factories, from mine shafts and from lighthouses, and from park benches and from all the dismal shelters of the unemployed.

Who are these millions who so variously come? Men and women, young and old, swarthy and pale, native and foreign-voiced, sickly and strong, hopeful and sullen, informed and ignorant—one could spin the differences endlessly.

I have but stated a theme: it is within the power of your imagination to give it what development you will. I am seeking merely to suggest something of the vastness, something of the infinite variegation, of the electoral phenomenon which marks our country today, from the Rio Grande to the Great Lakes, and from coast to coast.

What does it all mean?

One may answer easily that it is democracy in action on the largest scale the world has yet seen. But what really is democracy in action?

Today, and today alone, each voter is really sovereign. Today, in the act of choosing rulers, we ourselves rule. We are kings and queens for a day; and we deign to appoint our ministers. The curtained booth is our throne room, the pencil is our scepter, and the ballot is our proclamation.

An autocrat, having appointed his ministers, remains in power none the less and may change his ministers at his will. With us the case is very different. Our power once exercised, we abdicate; and for the next four years we are ruled by our own ministers. The exercise of our sovereignty, because of the very fact that it is so brief, because of the very fact that it is so long irrevocable in its results, has, therefore, an intensely critical importance.

It is not we who actually rule: democracy does not, cannot, mean that. Those who actually rule are, by necessity, few —infinitesimally few in proportion to the millions who vote. Those who rule constitute, inevitably, an oligarchy. Democracy means, in skeletal reality, the power to choose between oligarchies.

Yet that power, limited though it be, is to be cherished rather than despised. Think back two hundred years. Take your stand two hundred years ago in the slight civilized fringe of this country or in any one of the many older countries, eastern or western, which are represented here. From such a vantage, amid the oppression of regal or imperial absolutism, could you prophesy, could you imagine the doings of this day? And if you could, would not this day have seemed to you millennial? We know too well that the millennium lies far ahead; but the gain, none the less, is great beyond our reckoning.

For we do more than choose our oligarchy. We ask that the oligarchy we have chosen shall rule us, not for its own benefit, but for our benefit. Our asking, to be sure, does not suffice. Yet even our asking is, against the background of the centuries, audacious; and our asking—now granted, not thwarted—grows from faintness toward demand, wins on the whole an increasing measure of fulfillment.

Democracy, then, consists in a brief exercise of power, together with a long asking that the power we have conveyed be used for the common good.

How may we vitalize democracy? How guide and develop it toward a more perfect fulfillment of our common heart's desire? By making that long asking continuous, wise and insistent; by preparing ourselves more carefully for the critical brief exercise of power.

Before this day ends we shall have chosen the oligarchy which is to rule us for four years; but the powers of that oligarchy are not entirely beyond our influence. We have the right, constantly, to inquire whether their actions are in fact for the common good—a hard inquiry, to be pursued not in the spirit of partisanship, but in the spirit of research, not in a preconceived mood of hostility, but in recognition of the extreme inherent difficulty of the governmental process. And if we conclude that at this point or that the Government is betraying its trust, or that it is failing to seize some major opportunity for social advance, it is our right and our duty to express that conclusion, in such measure and through such channels as may be ours to use—through local political organizations, through direct communication with elected officers, through conversation, which may always ramify beyond our ken, through written articles or public speech, if indeed what we have to say is ripe for print or utterance.

Our asking, then, should be continuous; so should our preparation for the next exercise of our sovereignty. That next high moment of the marking of the ballot should represent no guesswork, no whim, no chance, no last-minute emotional conversion, no two-months' brevity of interest. It should represent a firm and sure decision, based equally upon long study and upon a constant and enlarging human friendliness. In our life as citizens the night of election day should mark not an end but a beginning.

Death of Dr. Will A. Hemingway

Dr. Will A. Hemingway '98, medical missionary under the American Board in Taiku, Shansi, China, and head of the Taiku Hospital, died November 8 after a week's illness with influenza and complications. He was fifty-eight years old.

Dr. Hemingway and his wife Mary Williams Hemingway '99 sailed for China in 1903, three years after the martyrs of the Boxer Uprising were buried in the Taiku Mission Compound, and plunged into the work of rebuilding the little community of scattered Christians.

The staff of the Taiku Hospital has increased under his administration to include, at the present time, one other American physician and two Chinese physicians, as well as a large corps of nurses, technicians, orderlies and other helpers, both Chinese and American. Dr. Hemingway also directed a health movement among the students in the mission and government schools, cooperating with the Chinese Health Society, and supervised the opening up of a branch hospital under a Chinese physician trained for fifteen years in the Taiku Hospital. In 1919 he was decorated by the Chinese Government for his success in stopping a terrible pneumonic plague epidemic known in the old days as the "Black Death"; and he has done similar work since then.

Dr. Hemingway was born in Oak Park, Ill., in 1874; was educated at Oberlin, Rush Medical School, and the Chicago Baptist Hospital and the Chicago Eye and Ear College. He married Mary E. Williams in 1903. He is survived by his wife, herself a third-generation missionary in China; by three daughters, Adelaide '28, Isabel '30 and Winifred, who is still in preparatory school in China. He leaves also a brother, George R. Hemingway of Oak Park, Ill., Acad. '94-'95; and two sisters, Mrs. F. B. Hines (Anginette B. Hemingway) '93, of Carbondale, Ill., and Mrs. C. G. Livingston (Grace Hemingway) '00-'02 of Honolulu.

Dr. Hemingway's last furlough was in the year 1927-28.

Political Aftermath

Lewis H. Pounds '82, Republican candidate for mayor in New York City, had the satisfaction of making a gallant if losing fight against Tammany. The interesting thing about the election was the great number of protest votes polled, even in the face of the general Democratic landslide. In addition to Mr. Pounds' 400,000 odd votes, the Socialist candidate polled well over 200,000, and over 100,000 votes were "written in" on the voting machines for Acting Mayor McKee, in spite of his announcement that he was not a candidate. A fusion ticket next fall should have a real chance.

Mr. Pounds has enjoyed notable support from the press. Even the Democratic *New York Times* expressed itself editorially (Oct. 29) as follows: "The voters have it in their power to effect genuine economy, and at the same time to bring about a better order in city affairs, by electing Mr. Pounds to office; or even by rolling up such a protest vote for him as to make smooth the path of fusion next Fall." The *New York Herald-Tribune* furnished warm and constant support. And the *Brooklyn Eagle*, the morning following the election, pronounced as its verdict: "Lewis H. Pounds, whose keen sense of civic duty prompted him to accept the Republican nomination, deserves unstinted praise for the campaign conducted by him. He made a dignified and telling effort . . . But Mr. Pounds was handicapped by the fact that the Republican party in this city has for so long been a mere appendage of Tammany Hall that independent voters have lost confidence in it.

"The Republican party never had a better opportunity to perform a real service in New York City, than that presented to it this year. The leaders threw away their chance. Mr. Pounds received but half-hearted support."

In the words of Mr. Pounds himself, in a letter written to President Wilkins, "A man who has had Oberlin training cannot shirk a moral responsibility wherever and whenever it appears, and with others I did feel that urge."

Charles A. Sawyer '08, candidate for Lieutenant-Governor of Ohio, was swept to victory over his Republican opponent Mr. Palmer.

The presidential vote in the community of Oberlin—Hoover 1789, Roosevelt 448, Norman Thomas 146—was not quite in line with the vote of the nation. Lorain County was the one county in Ohio electing a wholly Republican ticket.

STUDENT ACTIVITIES

Concerning the student vote, it is estimated by the Student Council that about 50% of those eligible to vote did so—a heartening response in view of the formalities necessary to secure absentee vot-

ing rights, etc. The leaders in the work felt amply repaid for the very real effort they had put forth. State and partisan clubs functioned vigorously; speakers were invited to Oberlin on student initiative; and open-air meetings and a political play diversified the scene.

Among the lighter incidents of the campaign was the arrest of six Oberlin students, members of the Oberlin Thomas-for-President Club but acting in no official capacity, by harassed police of the City of Lorain. The principle at stake, however, seemed to be not the Socialist platform but the right of free speech. Due to some Communist disturbances, the Lorain City Council had passed an ordinance requiring all who wished to hold a meeting in a public park (and presumably all other publicly owned property) to secure a permit from the mayor. The students applied twice for a permit to hold their Thomas rally, and were twice refused. The mayor said they might speak in a hall without interference, or on a privately owned lot; the students felt that the public parks were maintained by public funds and should therefore be open to free speech.

Two courses were open to the Oberlinites: applying for an injunction, which would suspend the ordinance for the one time only, or testing the constitutionality of the ruling by publicly reading excerpts setting forth the right of free speech. This latter course was adopted, and the meeting broken up and the six arrested by the police immediately after the constitutional excerpts so read.

The students once under arrest and freed on their own recognizance, Lorain was somewhat embarrassed to know what to do with them. The "offenders" favored trial by jury, but the city did not wish to incur the expense. At length the ordinance was amended over-night by abolishing the jail sentence formerly attached, and making the offense one to be tried before a municipal judge, with fines up to $200. The Oberlin students, after a lecture by police, were then set free and the case dismissed.

Two Socialist Party leaders who materialized during the initial excitement, also had themselves arrested by the same process, and expected to test the validity of the ordinance by standing trial.

The stand of the group won praise from the national Socialist Party, but the Lorain attitude is best expressed in the words of the editor of the *Lorain Journal:* "I am fully in sympathy with the fundamental principles of the thing, but I resent Lorain being used as a free speech laboratory." Editorial comment in the liberal papers, as typified by the *Toledo Blade:* "It has been stated else-

where in this paper and ought to be said again that the Lorain mayor who refused a permit to six Oberlin College students to hold a meeting advocating the election of Norman Thomas to the presidency is the kind of public official who is most responsible for creating out and out "reds" in this country. The right to free speech, provided by the constitution, has been the pride of this nation for nearly 150 years. The greatest preacher and teacher, Hugh Black, quoting Voltaire, once said in introducing Harry Emerson Fosdick, 'I don't agree with what you say but I will fight to give you the right to say it.' Doubtless I would not agree with all these Oberlin students might say about Norman Thomas and the Socialist program, but I am ready to fight to give them the right to say it—in the street or anywhere else."

Adviser to President-Elect

An actor if not a "lead" in one of the most interesting White House episodes of recent years was Professor Raymond Moley of Columbia, A.M. Oberlin '13, who accompanied President-elect Roosevelt on his informal discussion of foreign debt problems with President Hoover on November 22. President Hoover was accompanied only by Secretary of the Treasury Ogden L. Mills and Mr. Roosevelt only by Dr. Moley, who has long been adviser to the governor.

Homecoming Attendance Small

As perhaps to be expected in this centennial year, fewer alumni than usual seemed to be here for Homecoming, October 29. As far as the observation of the Alumni Office went, attendance was largely confined to a few of the faithful and to a fair number of younger graduates, many of whom had been attending N. E. O. T. A. in Cleveland.

Despite cold and threatening weather, the dormitories decorated bravely, Barr House (freshman men's asylum) winning the Alumni Cup with its smart fillip on Flit. Shurtleff, dipping Wooster in the well; French House, with its "Petit Theatre"; Red Lantern, gorily guillotining Wooster to the tune of getting a-head; and The Manor, with a complete miniature football field set-up, came in for honorable mention. The judges were Mrs. Harley L. Lutz (Rachel A. Young) '06; Francis Oakley '30 and Clayton Miller, returned Shansi representative, also '30. The Campus Restaurant won the business houses' Cup for the third time, earning it as their permanent possession.

Festivities of the day included an informal reception for alumni and parents following the game, and an All-College Dance in two sections—Warner Gymnasium and Men's Building—at night.

Artists Series, Faculty Recitals, Under Way

BY PROFESSOR JAMES HUSST HALL '14

The Artists Recitals Series opened the evening of October 25 with a concert by the Cleveland Symphony. The orchestra had already appeared in several programs at home and we profited by the somewhat later date of our first concert. The symphony chosen for the occasion was the Fourth by Tchaikovsky. The wistful, long-drawn melody of the second movement, and the continued *pizzicato* of the *Scherzo*, taken at a stunning tempo, were beautifully played, while the frequently enthusiastic brass section had plenty of opportunity to shine in the first and last movements. From the rest of the program we recall with especial pleasure the lovely horn melody in the *Nocturne* from the "Midsummer Night's Dream Music" by Mendelssohn—a treacherous score for the horn but played with precision and beauty, as was the rest of the program. We are looking forward to Cleveland's next concert on December 13 when they will give us an evening of Brahms and Wagner.

Of the illustrious names in music today perhaps none has the glamour of Lily Pons. This little French coloratura soprano has caught the fancy of the world and rightly so, for she brings to an art style that is fearfully lacking in content, a sincere musicianship potent to transfigure much that is bald and hollow. Lily Pons in her recital here on November 9 gave us a program ranging from Caccini, David and Donnizetti to our own day, represented by Zecchi. In the *Charmant Oiseau* and the *Mad Scene* we heard coloratura singing such as one dreams of and rarely, if ever, hears. This florid music has been turned by many a singer in our generation, often with ease and beauty, but I wonder if any in that audience the other evening had ever heard that degree of ease and beauty. Assisting artists were Mr. Bamboschek, pianist, and Mr. Van Leeuwen, flautist. The very reason for the choice of the flute as an *obbligato* to the voice in coloratura arias, seems to me valid for its exclusion as a solo instrument on the same program. But after all, the singer needs an intermission in a taxing program; and it is seldom that we hear flute solos as artistically played as were those at this concert. There was a large and enthusiastic audience, but even in a house with a $2.00 top (and I wonder how many times in the last two years Lily Pons has sung at such a price) a few seats still remained unsold.

Although a number of the faculty have appeared on the Wednesday evening recital programs this fall as well as in musical assemblies at the Chapel, the first full program to be given by a faculty member this year was a clarinet recital, in which Mr. George Waln was assisted by Mr. W. K. Breckenridge, pianist, and Mr. John Frazer, 'cellist. A *Sonata*, Op. 167, by Saint-Saëns, disclosed the variety of color that Mr. Waln secures, from the luscious, broad-flowing *cantabile* of the *chalumeau* to the clean-edged but not strident tones of the upper registers. A *Concertino* by Guildhaud, *Petite Pièce* by Debussy and *Fantasie Italienne* by Delmas followed. The final number was the Brahms *Trio*, Op. 114. The addition of the 'cello added a certain warmth and biting quality that acted as a fine foil, and the distinctive beauty of Mr. Waln's clarinet tone was enjoyed the more for the contrast in timbres. We are indebted to Mr. Waln for an evening of music that we seldom hear, and for a performance that was artistically satisfying.

Mr. Maurice Kessler gave an unusual viola recital in Warner Concert Hall on November 17. Two movements of a sonata by the Englishman, Forsyth, opened the program. In an *Adagio* from a Bruckner *String Quintet*, arranged by Mr. Kessler, Mr. Davis was at the organ. There was great charm in the next group of three compositions by old masters, played on the viola d'amore, and especially happy were we to have the opportunity of comparing the "color" of this instrument with that of the viola proper. After this delightful episode the choice of an idyllic *Légende* by Vierne was most happy, and the succeeding *Poème* of Jongen had great sweep and fine variety. The final number was the *Suite for viola and piano* by Ernest Bloch, bristling with originality and quite devoid of stereotyped phrases. It is impossible to catch the meaning of such music in first hearings; and yet the audience, still unaccustomed to the modern idiom (for we hear too little of present day music), felt the conviction and sincerity of the music through a sterling performance by Mr. Kessler and Mr. Skjerne.

The following evening Mr. Boris Rosenfield gave a piano recital, playing with fine clarity and keen sense of tonal contrast a well varied program. After the rich sonorities of a Brahms *Ballade* and *Intermezzo*, there came the sparkling and vivacious variations of Mozart on the French nursery tune, *Ah! Vous dirai-je maman*—a tune better known to many through the English parody, "Twinkle, twinkle little star"! Vividly juxtaposed to this light fabric, shot through with tinsel, were the Liszt variations on Bach's

Weinen, Klagen, massive and commanding. After the fine interpretation of Ravel's *Sonatine,* the Dohnanyi and Rubinstein numbers seemed less important. For the final group Mr. Rosenfield played the F minor *Ballade* and the F sharp minor *Polonaise,* and again the fusion of Chopin's poetic idea and form, unerringly fashioned for its medium, worked its magic. The program was played on the new Steinway concert grand, the finest, many feel, that we have had in the succession of these instruments on Warner Hall stage.

On one of the Wednesday evening recitals this past month the string sections of the Conservatory Orchestra played Bloch's *Concerto Grosso,* under the direction of Mr. Maurice Kessler. This was undoubtedly the best performance we have heard from the orchestra. The rather recent and very rapid rise of the string department has been noted before, but never before have we had so many fine string players in Oberlin. Despite the complexities of the score the intonation and ensemble were markedly good. The pathos of the slow movement, and the incisiveness of the final fugue that swept all before it, will be long remembered.

Pirandello Play to be Given

The rather subtle play, "Six Characters in Search of an Author," by the Italian Luigi Pirandello, is the choice of the Oberlin Dramatic Association for their fall performance, the evenings of December 2 and 3. The play is being coached by Professor R. A. Jelliffe of the English Department.

The choice of Pirandello marks the continuation of the Dramatic Association's policy of last year, which, in "The Cradle Song," brought to its Oberlin audience another of the modern continental dramas.

"Six Characters in Search of an Author," first produced ten years ago, is a subtle study of the conflict between illusion and reality. It is here represented by the characters of a play who have been brought into existence by their artist-creator and who, once created, take matters into their own hands and project for themselves the curve of reality their author has begun.

On November 4 and 5, the Dramatic Association undertook the interesting experiment of staging, in Finney Chapel, two performances of negro plays, played by the Gilpin Players of Cleveland. Daniel Reed's stage adaption of Julia Peterkin's novel, "Scarlet Sister Mary," was given the first evening, and "In Abraham's Bosom," the 1927 Pulitzer Prize Play by Paul Green, the second.

The Gilpin Players, although a strictly amateur organization, are already recognized as perhaps the outstanding group of negro players in the country.

Student Employment

Over half the men on the Campus, this fall, and practically a third of the women, are engaging in some sort of remunerative work in addition to their studies.

No less than seventy-one percent of the men of the junior class are finding it necessary to earn money to help pay college expenses. Sixty-nine percent hold regular jobs, which represents some sort of steady "income" or its equivalent going to eighty-five men.

The senior men hold second place, with sixty-nine percent earning some money and sixty-six percent earning "regular" money. Sixty percent of the sophomore men are helping themselves in some measure, and forty percent of the freshmen. Doubtless more freshmen would like work, were there more work to do.

An interesting angle of the "job" situation on the Campus is the way in which regular employment tends to go to upperclassmen. Of course by far the greatest proportion of regular jobs are those for board and room, which are generally arranged for in the spring. In both the junior and the senior classes, but a negligible percent of the men work at odd jobs. In the sophomore class, over eleven percent of the working men find nothing but odd jobs; among the freshmen, thirteen percent.

Total employment percentages for women in the College of Arts and Sciences are as follows: senior, 47.27; junior, 42.75; sophomore, 40.48; and freshman, 16.46.

A rather serious aspect of the situation is the scarcity of employment, during the summer of 1932, as compared with the summer of 1931. In 1931, 63% of the men in the College of Arts and Sciences, and 32% of the women, were able to find summer work. In 1932, but 45% of the men, and 22% of the women worked during vacation. On the Campus as a whole, including the Conservatory and the Graduate School of Theology, 57% of the men and 28% of the women worked during the summer of 1931. The drop to last year's total—41% of the men and 20% of the women—would prophesy the greatly increased need for employment, on the part of many students, during the school year itself.

Former Contractor Dies

George Feick, Sr., the builder of Severance Chemical Laboratory, Carnegie Library, Finney Chapel, the Administration Building and the Men's Building, died in Sandusky November 12. He was 83 years old.

Fourth Cross-Country Crown

After a seemingly smashing defeat (21-35) by Wooster's Scots October 29, the Oberlin harriers came back two weeks later to win their fourth consecutive Big Six Championship at Muskingum by the slender margin of one point. The finish was the closest and most exciting since 1929 when the Crimson and Gold captured its first O. I. A. crown. Realizing that she needed all the breaks, Oberlin took the Muskingum hills smartly and fought valiantly on the final stretch. The score at the finish was Oberlin 31, Wooster 32 and Muskingum 61. Individually and as a team the Yeomen ran way over their heads, each man bettering his best previous time. Deciding factor in the meet was the sudden burst of speed in the last quarter-mile that gave Oberlin sixth and seventh places instead of seventh and eighth.

Coach Kinsey's men placed as follows: Captain Dublo '34, second (actually third, but Schindler, who took second, was Mt. Union's only entry and therefore disregarded in team honors); Bauer '33, fifth; Lightner '33, sixth; Schwinn, a sophomore, seventh; Smith '33, last scoring Yeomen, twelfth.

In the last meet of the season, November 19, the Crimson and Gold swamped Case harriers 15-45. Bauer, Dublo, Schwinn and Smith came in abreast to take the first four places. Lightner came in fifth; McSweeney '34 sixth. The first Case runner finished seventh.

Hobbs Resign as Managers of Inn

After several years as managers of the Oberlin Inn, Mr. and Mrs. W. D. Hobbs are severing their connections with the local hotel at the end of November. Mrs. Mary Brand Ruggles (P. T. '99) will assume the management of the Inn and will continue to operate the dining room as at present.

Mr. Hobbs' name has long been associated with good things to eat. Nearly thirty years ago he started a restaurant on East College street which was famous in its day.

As managers of the Inn both he and his wife have made friends throughout a wide area for their courteous treatment and splendid dining room service.

Mrs. Ruggles has lived for a number of years in New York, where she was engaged in several large business enterprises. She returned to Oberlin some months ago to be with her invalid mother, Mrs. Julia Brand, and recently opened the Carlyle Gift Shop in one of the rooms at the Inn. She will retain her interests in this shop while serving as hotel manager.

Athletic Interests of Freshman Men

Swimming, not football, is the sport arousing most interest among the men of '36 according to Dr. J. Herbert Nichols '11 in his survey of the athletic interests and high school participation of the freshmen men this fall.

Next to swimming, tennis, with 104 devotees, is most popular.

Out of 156 men, 142 or 90% can swim; 132 or 85% list it as one of their preferred sports; 28, or 18%, have passed the Red Cross Life Saving Test.

The percentage of freshman men interested in football has taken a sudden leap as compared with last year—36% for 1932 against 18% in 1931. The percentage of those entering who have made their high-school team, however, is almost cut in half—10% this year as against 19% last. Total percentage of interest and participation, 46% in 1932; 37% in 1931.

Basketball is slightly more popular with '36 than it was with '35. This year, 40% or 62 men are interested, although they have never participated or made their high-school team; an additional 15% come with high-school experience. The comparative figures last fall were 36% merely interested or new to the game, and 14% with experience.

Of the two other major varsity sports, baseball and track, percentage of interest and experience runs about the same as last year's. A greater percentage of boys show interest in track; a less percentage than in last year's class, apparently, have taken part in high-school track events.

Golf takes seventh place on the list as a preferred sport with 42 men, following, in order, swimming, tennis, basketball, football, baseball and track.

Mrs. Penfield Celebrates 95th Birthday

Mrs. Sarah Hoyt Penfield '58, earliest living graduate of Oberlin College (though not the oldest) celebrated her ninety-fifth birthday at her home in New York City on October 28. Flowers, cards and other remembrances from friends made a gala two-days' celebration for her.

Mrs. Penfield, who visited St. Augustine, Florida, this past August, is fairly well, cheerful, and hopes to greet her friends at the Centennial Homecoming in June. She is interested in old and new things, reads her paper every morning, and expected to vote for Hoover November 8! Her friends wish her many more happy birthdays, which are celebrations, not only for her, but for Oberlin.

Hard Football Season Over

Oberlin ended her unlucky 1932 grid season with a 14 to o defeat at the hands of Cleveland's Case, Saturday, November 19. Considering that this year's Rough Riders were one of the best teams Case has ever put out, the score itself was not heart-breaking. Case had been allowed a more generous margin of touchdowns.

The Yeomen have at no time figured as a "push-over," however handicapped by a dearth of experienced first-string material and a constantly mounting toll of injuries. Losing, before the season ever began, two of their brightest sophomore hopes, their captain and their only experienced end, they subsequently dropped Frank Barry, first class backfield man; Jack Kennedy, the remaining veteran lineman, effective tackle and acting captain; and—the Tuesday before the Case game—Bruce Brickley, diminutive punting star. Under these circumstances it is easy to understand that while the team has fought every game through to the bitter finish, it has not consistently experienced that roseate glow of confidence which is the mother of victories.

Coach Lysle Butler likewise deserves all credit for a gallant fight, closing up the ranks after each casualty and carrying on with what was left. His almost totally inexperienced squad has made no bad showing, and furnishes substantially better hopes for 1933.

Summary of the season: out of eight games, two won, six lost. Out of the lost games, three went by "breaks"—the Rochester safety, the Wooster touchdown, and the two fumbles in the Denison game. Case, Reserve plus Finnigan and the veteran Otterbein squad were really more powerful outfits. Oberlin did not win a home game, had the misfortune not to make a touchdown on her own field. Total points made by Oberlin—27; total by opponents—93.

WOOSTER 6, OBERLIN 0

The Homecoming game with Wooster was perhaps the hardest of the season for Oberlin to lose. The Scots had given Case plenty of trouble a week or so earlier, but were considerably weaker than the aggregation that Oberlin had outfaced 13 to 12 last year.

Oberlin outplayed Wooster consistently in the first half, gaining over the visitors almost three to one and three times threatening the Scots' goal. Oberlin's first scoring threat came soon after the starter's gun, when a bad Wooster punt gave her the ball on Wooster's 18-yard stripe, only to lose it on downs. Shortly after, the Crimson and Gold, starting from its own 47, marched to the Wooster 23-yard line and there lost the ball on a fumble. Another fumble, this time by Wooster on their own 20, gave Oberlin the ball; the Yeomen made one first down, but were unable to supply the last-minute dynamite.

After the half, the Wooster offense began to click. Recovering an Oberlin fumble on their own 30-yard line, the Scots took the oval up the field to the Oberlin 4-yard mark, and on the fourth down, went over for the score.

Both teams were hampered by numb fingers; and kicking against the gale that swept down the field was all but impossible.

OBERLIN 7, ALLEGHENY 6

Meeting a team almost as luckless, this season, as themselves, the Yeomen took the unfortunate Alligators in tow at Meadville on November 5. Oberlin's one-point margin resulted from a partially blocked 'Gator place-kick by Tackle Hinz '35.

The Yeomen scored in the second quarter, when Ruth intercepted a long pass and returned the ball to his own 45-yard line. Successive passes took it to the Allegheny 4-yard line, where Sams carried it over the goal on the fourth play after Allegheny had repeatedly charged offside in an effort to stall. Oberlin refused the penalty, and Brickley passed to Ruth for the extra point.

Allegheny scored in the third quarter, after Sams had kicked out on his own 42. The touchdown was made on a pass; a moment after, Hinz blocked the kick that would have meant a tie.

The game was hard-fought, and featured by daring passing and long runs on the part of both teams.

DENISON 8, OBERLIN 0

On a day so cold that both teams were watching for the breaks sure to come from slippery field and freezing hands, Denison managed to convert two critical Oberlin fumbles during the second half into a touchdown and a safety. Denison outplayed Oberlin on ground gained, but was repeatedly held at bay by the superior punting of Brickley and Sams. Oberlin did not really threaten at any time during the game, her nearest approach to the enemy's goal following Shaw's recovery of a Denison fumble on the latter's 26-yard line.

The Big Reds made several threats during the first half, Oberlin defense stiffening against their most determined attack on her own 12-yard line. In the third period, Denison got the ball on an intercepted pass, and punted to the Oberlin ten-yard mark. Brickley, attempting to punt out of danger, fumbled, and had to fall on the ball to give the visitors a safety. A few minutes later in a similar situation Sams also fumbled and Denison recovered on Oberlin's three-yard line. The third drive for goal brought the touchdown. A desperate Oberlin aerial attack failed to take hold.

CASE 14, OBERLIN 0

Playing on a snow-covered field, the Yeomen went down before Case 14 to 0 in the final game of the season. The defeat was generally anticipated, and the score against Oberlin smaller than many expected.

Case scored in the first minutes of the second quarter, driving through center after a brillant offense had landed the Scientists on the Oberlin 2-yard stripe.

The third quarter ended 7-0, but at the beginning of the fourth period Case ran back one of Sams' punts, and a long succeeding run brought them to Oberlin's one-yard line. The touchdown came on the next play.

Sams' kicking was Oberlin's best defense and one of the most remarkable features of the game. Brickley, his co-star in the previous games of the season, had been operated upon for acute appendicitis five days before the game.

PROSPECTS FOR 1933

Oberlin's prospects for another year look rather better. Butler will have thirteen lettermen for nucleus as against six this fall; of which six only two finished out the season.

Dean Ruth '34, stocky, hard-hitting back from Cincinnati, is hailed as Oberlin's 1933 Captain-elect. Dean has not himself greatly frequented the limelight in the last two years, preferring rather to make the glare possible for others. Winning his first varsity letter in his sophomore year, he is easily the cleanest and hardest blocker in the backfield, and will doubtless be Butler's mainstay next season behind the line. Ruth played fullback last year and this season has had some experience at quarter.

Besides Ruth, Butler will have Punter Brickley, Center Brown, Backs Correll and Smith, and Linemen Berry, Edwards, Hinz, Morse, Shaw, Whitmer and Woodward, all of whom won their letters for the first time this fall. Jack Kennedy '35 at tackle wins his second letter; lettermen lost by graduation in June will be Captain Elmer Barker, Frank Barry and Henry Sams.

Potential football material from the class of 1936 is not as extensive as everyone had hoped, but what there is will fit nicely into Butler's scheme. Hopefuls include a couple of ends and some welcome backfield material. A few sophomore backs and linemen ought to ripen over the winter, also. On which cheering note, hail and farewell!

Campaigned in Indiana

Miss Clara Gilbert '01 received personal commendation from the Indiana Republican State Central Committee for her active participation in Indiana's Republican campaign just past. Her work included traveling long hours from county to county, organizing and making speeches, and broadcasting over station WKBF for the G. O. P.

News of the Faculty

With the school year well under way, the open season for faculty extra-curricular activities and publications begins.

Professor Karl F. Geiser of the Political Science Department has a published article, "Hitler's Hold on Germany," in one of the early November issues of *The Nation.* Dr. Geiser spent the summer in Germany studying political conditions, and was especially interested in the strength of the Hitler movement. He spoke October 25 before the Congregational Men's Club of Lorain, and October 27 before the Congregational Men's Club of Elyria, on his experiences.

Dean Thomas W. Graham was invited to take part in the recognition service for the Rev. L. A. Owen, new pastor of the First Congregational Church in Iowa City, Iowa, on November 20. On October 21, Dean Graham was present at the dedication of the new Rochester-Colgate Divinity School at Colgate University. Sunday, October 23 he attended the Ohio Conference of Religious Education at Springfield, addressing the Sunday morning session of the conference.

Professor G. Walter Fiske gave a recent address before the student body of Hiram College, and also two lectures in the Department of Religious Education there. At the session of the national Commission on Worship held in New York City recently, Dr. Fiske gave the opening address on "The Cultural Lag in Rural Worship." This Commission is one of the activities of the Federal Council of Churches of Christ in America.

Miss Marian Shaw, who was head Cataloguer of the College Library from 1923 to 1926, has been at work for the past two years on an important publication, "Essay and General Literature Index," for the H. W. Wilson Co. She has completed four out of a projected six volumes.

Dr. Harry N. Holmes, head of the Chemistry Department, recently delivered two addresses on "Catalysis and Colloid Chemistry," the first at the University of Tennessee, Knoxville, Tenn., October 27, and the second before the Atlanta Section of the American Chemical Society at Atlanta, Ga., the following day. On November 15 he lectured before the Detroit Section of the American Chemical Society on "Some Recent Applications of Colloid Chemistry"; and on November 25 addressed the Science and Mathematics Association at its national meeting in Cleveland on "The Relation of Colloid Chemistry to Medicine." Dr. Crile, Cleveland surgeon, was also on the program.

Professor Newell L. Sims spoke on his experiences in Russia this summer before the Lorain County Social Workers on November 7.

Professor R. P. Jameson's handbook of French culture, *Le Cercle Français,* came from press (D. C. Heath and Co.) October 28. *Le Cercle Français* is not only a manual for French clubs; it contains also extensive general bibliographies, dealing with the conversation, history and culture of the French nation.

Professor K. W. Gehrkens of the School Music Department attended the meetings of the executive committee of the Music Supervisors' National Conference last month. The executive committee has entire charge of the planning of the music education program for Chicago's Century of Progress exposition to be held next summer. Professor Gehrkens spent October 21-25 in Greensboro, North Carolina and Washington, D. C. In Greensboro he gave several addresses before a group of music teachers and supervisors from the entire state of North Carolina, and also gave an address before an association of school superintendents. In Washington he conferred with Carl Engel of the Library of Congress and other music leaders about the meeting of the Music Teachers' National Association to be held in Washington in December.

Dr. W. F. Bohn attended the meetings of the Congregational Educational Society, in session in Chicago during the week of October 24.

President Ernest H. Wilkins was in New York City November 15-18, attending the celebrated three-day conference at New York University on "The Obligations of Universities to the Social Order." This convention recalled the convention of a hundred years ago, at which the leading educators of the day proffered their advice on the initial undertaking of the University. Dr. Wilkins was a member of the conference advisory committee. Dr. Luther Gulick, Oberlin '14, and Director of the National Institute of Public Administration, was among the distinguished speakers.

Dr. Wilkins spoke at Dana College Tuesday, November 15, on "The Opportunity of a New College." The evening of Thursday, November 17, he and Dr. H. H. K'ung '06 were the guests of honor at the annual Alumni Dinner in New York.

William H. Seaman, Director of Admissions, and Francis Oakley attended the meeting of the Association of Ohio College Field Secretaries, held November 17 in Toledo, and the meetings of the Association of Ohio College Registrars and Examiners, held the following day.

Donald M. Love, Registrar, spoke on "Oberlin's Experience with the Ranking System" at one session of the Ohio College Registrars and Examiners' Convention at Toledo. Two years ago he addressed the Association on the plans for the proposed ranking system here, and his paper this year was a follow-up of the same subject, and a report on some of the results. Mr. Love was elected vice-president of the Association for the coming year.

Professor Harvey Wooster of the Economics Department spoke before the faculty of Baldwin-Wallace College November 4, on "The Curriculum as a Tool in the Educative Process." The invitation to speak came as a result of an article published in *The Journal of Higher Education* for October, in which Dr. Wooster advocates material changes in the curriculum of the liberal arts college.

Dr. H. A. Miller, former professor of sociology in the College, conducted, November 11-18, an intensive seminar on world movements at Ashland Folk School, Grant, Michigan. Teachers, ministers, social workers, foreign students and others interested in the study of social and economic change, attended.

Armstrong Secretary of New Hampshire Conference

Rev. Robert G. Armstrong '12, Theol. '14, was formally installed as Secretary of the New Hampshire (Congregational) Conference at an induction service held October 27 at Concord. He succeeds Dr. Edward R. Stearns, who has held the post of conference secretary for twenty years.

Rev. Dwight J. Bradley '12, of Newton, Mass., preached the induction sermon on the theme, "Our Apostolic Ministry."

Secretary Armstrong enters upon his work as head of the New Hampshire Conference after a fruitful ministry, first at Amherst, Ohio, then at Spencer, Mass.; Buffalo, N. Y.; Westville, N. Y.; and the South Church, Pittsfield, Mass.

Host to Northern Ohio Organists Guild

Meeting outside of Cleveland for the first time in its history, the Northern Ohio Chapter of the American Guild of Organists held its November meeting in Oberlin on November 22, as the guest of the organ faculty of the Conservatory of Music. The program of the evening was played on three different organs—the two-manual Estey in Fairchild Chapel, the four-manual Skinner in Finney Chapel, and the three-manual Skinner in Warner Concert Hall. The performers were, in order, Mr. George O. Lillich, Mr. Bruce Davis, assisted by the A Cappella Choir, and Mr. Leo C. Holden. The Conservatory Elizabethan Singers also assisted, singing a group of carols.

Preceding the program, a supper was held at the Inn.

Represent Oberlin at Other Schools

According to the Annual Report of the President submitted to the Trustees in November, seventeen alumni have served as official delegates of the College at academic functions of various sorts during 1931-32. The representatives and the occasions have been as follows:

Dr. J. R. Rogers '75, at the inauguration of Dr. F. L. Babbott, Jr., as President of Long Island College of Medicine.

Dr. G. W. Mead '91, at the inauguration of Dr. C. A. Anderson as President of Tusculum College.

Dr. E. D. Durand '93, at the Centennial Celebration of the University of Richmond.

Dr. J. H. McMurray '97, at the inauguration of Dr. R. W. Lloyd as President of Maryville College.

Mrs. F. P. Ensminger '98, at the inauguration of Dr. D. R. Anderson as President of Wesleyan College, Macon, Georgia.

Dr. Edgar Fauver '99, at the Centennial Celebration of Wesleyan University.

Mr. J. E. Stannard '00, at the inauguration of Dr. W. A. Boylan as President of Brooklyn College.

Dr. C. H. Birdseye '01, at the Centennial Celebration of Gettysburg College.

Dr. W. F. Bohn '01, at the Centennial Celebration of Lafayette College.

Miss Clara Gilbert '01, at the inauguration of Dr. W. H. Athern as President of Butler University.

Mr. H. L. Rawdon '04, at the George Washington Bicentennial Convocation at George Washington University.

Dr. Grove Patterson '05, at the inauguration of Dr. W. V. Lytle as President of Defiance College.

Mr. C. W. Hunt '09, at the inauguration of Dr. K. T. Waugh as President of Dickinson College.

Judge E. H. Van Fossan '09, at the inauguration of Dr. D. H. Gordon as President of St. John's College.

Mr. P. E. Grosh, Cons. '20, at the dedication of Harbison Chapel, the Hall of Science and the Frances St. Leger Babcock Organ of Grove City College.

Mr. S. S. Isseks '22, at the first College Commencement exercises of Yeshiva College.

Mr. R. L. Sutherland, A.M. '27, at the inauguration of Dr. H. P. Rainey as President of Bucknell University.

Alumni who have so far this year acted as official representatives of Oberlin at similar functions are:

Mr. Harry A. Ford '98, representing Oberlin at the dedication of the Edward L. Doheny, Jr., Memorial Library of the University of Southern California on September 12.

Mr. Robert E. Ewalt '07, at the dedication of the Mary Reed Library of the University of Denver on October 28.

Dr. Raymond Accepts Atlanta Post

Dr. C. Rexford Raymond '95, Seminary '00, for the last five years pastor of Pilgrim Congregational Church in Chattanooga, Tennessee, has resigned his pastorate to accept the chair of Church Administration in the Atlantic Theological Seminary Foundation, affiliated with the School of Religion at Vanderbilt University, Nashville, Tenn. He will enter upon his new duties January 1.

The Foundation has recently launched a campaign for $200,000 additional endowment, and Dr. Raymond will serve as Director of that campaign. Commenting editorially upon his resignation, the *Chattanooga News* says: "Chattanoogans, regardless of religious beliefs, will regret that Dr. C. Rexford Raymond . . . has resigned . .

"While in Chattanooga, Dr. Raymond has been a liberal in religion, and a worker in all movements having to do with public welfare. The church, he believes, has a great social duty as well as a religious one. He is popular in all circles . . . and respected universally among our people."

Curtis-Oberlin Reunion

A reunion of the Curtis family, which turned out incidentally to be an Oberlin reunion, was held at Moorestown, N. J., last August. The guest of honor was Edith Curtis '10, returned from Japan on furlough. Others present were: Otis Curtis '11, Lucy Weeks Curtis '13 and their children, Otis Jr. '36, Edgar and Margaret Anne of Ithaca, N. Y.; Ruth Curtis Lewis '18 and William D. Lewis '19 of Newark, Del.; Ethel Metcalf Curtis ex'23, Howard Curtis '15 and their children Howard Metcalf and Virginia; and Anna Schmidt, Conservatory '32, of Moorestown, New Jersey.

Edith Curtis' present address is 25 Amstel Ave., Newark, Del.

Monument at Kitty Hawk

A monument to Wilbur and Orville Wright, aviation pioneers, erected by authority of Congress, was unveiled at Kitty Hawk, North Carolina, on Saturday, November 19. The sixty-foot three-cornered shaft, two sides of which are carved in conventional wing-design, marks the site where in 1903 a heavier-than-air craft was flown for the first time in history.

The Wright brothers are related to Oberlin through their sister Katharine Wright Haskell '98, who died March 3, 1929.

Peace Study Groups

Russia has lost none of her glamour, and present conditions in Germany are scarcely less interesting, according to returns from the study-group questionnaire sent out by the Peace Society last month. Twenty-six percent of those replying chose Russia as their particular field of interest; eighteen percent will study Germany. Austria was the only country who failed to receive a single vote.

The Peace Society expects to get its thirteen study-groups organized and well under way before the Christmas holidays.

Former Y. M. C. A. Head Becomes President of Muskingum

Dr. Robert N. Montgomery, who will be remembered as Y. M. C. A. Secretary in Oberlin during 1921-22 and the husband of Ruth Kelley Montgomery, Conservatory '22, was installed as President of Muskingum College on November 11. The date marked the twenty-eighth anniversary of his father's inauguration as president of the same institution in 1904. His brother, J. Knox Montgomery, Jr., who served as acting head of Muskingum last year, becomes executive vice-president. Formal inauguration services will be held in the spring.

Dr. Montgomery was hailed as "America's youngest college president" on his election, two years ago, to the presidency of Tarkio College, Tarkio, Mo., at the age of 30 years. He is still the youngest at 32, his "rival," Dr. Robert Hutchins of Chicago University, being 33.

After leaving Oberlin, Dr. Montgomery went to Pittsburgh Theological Seminary and graduated with the highest honors. He won a year's scholarship at the University of Edinburough, and on his return, at the age of twenty-seven, was elected to the chair of Hebrew and Old Testament literature at the Pittsburgh Seminary. From Pittsburgh he went to Tarkio.

Art Museum Exhibitions

An exhibition of eighty-six watercolors, by the same number of international artists, was the display at the Allen Art Museum during most of the month of November. The exhibition featured work done in the modern spirit and aroused much comment among the visitors.

An exhibition of superb facsimile reproductions of the paintings by Pieter Breughel in the Vienna gallery forms the exhibit for December.

Retires From American Board

Mrs. Lydia Lord Davis, executive secretary of the Oberlin-Shansi Memorial Association, retired from her position as thank-offering secretary to the Women's Board of the Interior, and as assistant secretary in the Home Department of the American Board of Foreign Missions, at the Board's meeting in late October. She plans, however, to continue her work with Oberlin and the Shansi Association, with which she has been connected since its organization in 1907.

Early Graduate Honored

One of Oberlin's earliest graduates was honored this month when the Congregational Church in Hillsboro, Oregon, celebrated the 125th birthday anniversary of John S. Griffin t'38, founder of the Hillsboro church and of Congregationalism in the State of Oregon. The celebration lasted an entire week, November 16 through Thanksgiving.

After his graduation from Oberlin Father Griffin (as he was known in Oregon) was sent as missionary to the West by the North Litchfield, Connecticut, Association. After two attempts to found missions among the Snake Indians, and a winter spent as chaplain at Fort Vancouver, he pushed on and settled on the Tualatin Plains in the spring of 1841. There the first Congregational service for white people to be held west of the Rocky Mountains was conducted by Father Griffin in that same year. Mrs. Griffin was the first white woman to come into that part of the country. The church founded in 1841 was the lineal predecessor of the Hillsboro Congregational Church, and the first Congregational church in the state.

Father Griffin died at Hillsboro in 1899, at the age of 92 years.

As part of the celebration the Oberlin Chapter of Oregon was invited to hold an "Oberlin Night" on November 18. Magnus G. Riebeling of Portland, acad. '97-'00, gave the first address. "Oberlin's training in the ideals of self-government was a great factor in the action of the Rev. Mr. Griffin at the Champoeg Meeting (1843)," he said. "The relationship of good citizenship and religion has always been a part of the College's impression upon its students." The Rev. John S. Edmunds of Portland, '80 and t'83, spoke next on "Oberlin—Past and Present."

Music was furnished by Miss Elfrieda Riebeling, daughter of Mr. Magnus G. Riebeling, Mrs. Juanita Kilborn Clauss (Cons. 1910-13) and Mrs. Erma Taylor Sparks (Cons. '12). Mrs. Clauss sang two of her own compositions.

Greetings came to the meeting from the Forest Grove Congregational Church, Forest Grove, Oregon, which was founded in 1845 by a small group of members from the original Hillsboro church. Miss Nellie Allen Cole, acad. '03-'04, College '08-'10 and k'09, a member of the Forest Grove church, accompanied the pastor to give the message. The evening's program was arranged by Mrs. Courtland L. Booth (Juanita Snyder) '08.

At the formal service in Hillsboro Congregational Church Sunday, November 20, Oberlin was represented by Dr. Henry L. Bates '76.

Telegrams of congratulation were received from President Hoover and President-elect Roosevelt, and official letters of recognition and congratulation from Governor Meier of Oregon and from many church leaders, including Dr. S. Parkes Cadman, radio preacher of the Federal Council, and Dr. Carl S. Patton, Oberlin '88, moderator of the Congregational National Council.

Washington Women's Club Meets

A November luncheon-meeting of the Washington Oberlin Women's Club was held on Monday, November 14. Those present were Mrs. Lowell Kilgore (Helen Ford) '25, President, Mrs. Frederick F. Blachly (Miriam Oatman) '12, Ruth Bliss Buddington '26, Ethel Hastings Gott, Cons. '15-'16, Gladys Rowley Gunn '21, Mrs. John P. M. Metcalf (Caroline Post) '85, Irene Richards '13 and Billy Millard Bayliss k'26. After lunch, Dr. Purse of the Y. W. C. A. spoke to the group about the health work of her organization. Plans were made for entertaining Mrs. George W. Andrews at the December meeting.

R. M. B.

Grand Rapids Elects Officers

The Grand Rapids, Michigan, Oberlin Club spent a very enjoyable evening, Saturday, October 29, at the home of Mr. and Mrs. Fred Slack '16. A pot-luck supper was followed by a business meeting. The newly elected officers are: President, Harold Tower, Cons. '11; Sec.-Treas., Mrs. Carter Christiancy (Florence Bennett) '18; and Social Chairman, Fred Slack. New members were Charles Vogan Cons. '32 and Jack Hardy '30. The group, including plenty of children, numbered twenty-five. Much enthusiasm was shown in a good old-fashioned "sing" with Charles Vogan at the piano and Florence Christiancy whistling.

Oberlin names present: Andrus, Blake, Vogan, Christiancy, Hardy, Herz, Johnson, Mapes, Skidmore, Slack.

D. S. B.

Chicago Women Meet

For the third successive year, a speaker from Oberlin addressed the October meeting of the Oberlin Women's Club of Chicago, which was held Saturday afternoon, October 8. The Club met in Ida Noyes Hall of the University of Chicago to hear Dr. Frederick B. Artz speak on "European History as Reflected in the Work of the Great Tapestry Makers of the Middle Ages and Renaissance." The lecture was illustrated by lantern slides which certainly reflected the history of the period, especially when interpreted by Dr. Artz's interesting and witty comments. He also spoke briefly of conditions in the College, and—even though this is the fall of 1932—he was able to find several favorable items to report.

Chicago Musicale

The hospitality of Mrs. C. E. Hemingway of Oak Park made it possible for the Oberlin alumnae of Chicago and their guests to enjoy, Saturday, November 19, a charming musicale in her home. Amid most artistic surroundings, the beautiful paintings of our hostess greeting us at every turn in the huge studio living room, it proved indeed a memorable occasion. Mercy Hooker '13, President of the group, also acted as hostess, and Helen Smails Swearingen '13 was in charge of the program.

The artists were Miss Helen Nightingale, soprano, Miss Fannie Fine, violinist, and Helen Swearingen, accompanist and pianist. Miss Nightingale veritably lived up to her name, her singing of the Verdi aria being marked by bird-like clearness and ease. Miss Fine did some excellent violin playing, and our own program chairman delighted us with a splendid group of piano numbers, rendered in a highly individual and refreshingly artistic manner.

The artists received much applause and many requests for encores; and everyone voted it an outstanding event in the musical affairs of the Association.

A. B. S.

Conducts Radio Choir

Dr. R. Nathaniel Dett, Cons. '08, honorary Mus. D. Oberlin '26, is directing a group known as the American Choir, which broadcasts over station WHAM, Rochester, N. Y.

Dr. Dett is internationally known as a composer and conductor, and was director of the Hampton Institute Choir during its strikingly successful foreign tour in 1930.

The American Choir, a group of sixteen voices, made its debut in September over a coast-to-coast N. B. C. network. It began a new broadcast series November 1.

News of Alumni

'78—General Wilder S. Metcalf of Lawrence, Kansas, has been appointed Chairman of the Board of Directors of the Federal Home Loan Bank for the Topeka District. General Metcalf served in the Philippine War and in the World War. He was the U. S. Pension Agent for the Topeka District for twelve years, Commander of the Kansas State American Legion for ten years and has also been Chairman of the National Finance Committee of the American Legion.

'82—Word has been received from Pinetop, Arizona, of the death of Sina E. Burtt.

'84—Mrs. William E. Fuller (Frances H. Ensign) has resigned her position as State Treasurer of the Ohio Women's Christian Temperance Union. She has served in every official capacity of that organization, and has been treasurer for the past 38 years. Mrs. Fuller is known far and wide for her outstanding speeches on the dry subject.

'85, '86—Rev. and Mrs. Harry D. Sheldon (Grace Safford) have been spending the past few months with Professor and Mrs. Wayne Manning (Margaret Sheldon), both members of the Class of '20 in Northampton, Mass., where Professor Manning is on the faculty of Smith College. They made a short visit to Ohio in August. Mr. Sheldon resigned his pastorate of Rugby Congregational Church, Brooklyn, N. Y., about a year ago. Their address is 14 Adair Street, Northampton, Mass.

'89—Harriet Cumming Gustin lives in Jackson Heights, Long Island, and plays 24 holes of golf every day, weather permitting. She spent part of the summer in Pocasset on Cape Cod. Mrs. Gustin reports seeing other Oberlinites recently: Jessie Wilcox Gurney acad., Fred W. Gurney '91, Roma Sexton Gurney '26, John E. Gurney '24 and Maude Tucker Doolittle '91.

'90—F. I. Carruthers, Advertising Manager of the *Denver Post,* is celebrating his 42nd year in the newspaper business. He advises us that he "would like to see more items in the Alumni Magazine of graduates of '89, '90 and '91." He enjoyed a visit with "Bob" Millikan '91 at the Cactus Club in Denver last summer.

'90—Carrie Winter Kofoid spoke at the Pacific Slope Congress of Congregational Churches at San Diego in October on a subject reflecting her active interest in church work.

ex'93—Abel Kimball has been elected Treasurer of Lake County, Ohio, by the largest vote given any candidate on the County ticket. He has been in the hardware business in Madison, Ohio, for many years.

'93—Florence M. Snell is returning to this country "for good" from South Africa where for a number of years she has been teaching at Huguenot University College in Wellington, Cape Province, the only women's college in South Africa. Her address for the present is in care of Mrs. John Russell, Jr., Stone Farm, Greenfield, Mass.

'96—Mae Emery White is teaching materia medica and therapeutics in the Mercy Hospital School of Nursing. She is also doing special work in anaesthesia and medical practice for girls and women. Her husband, Dr. William A. White, is practicing general medicine. They have two children: Margaret ex'34 who is now a junior at Antioch College and William, a freshman at Mt. Union College.

'99—Andrew W. Williamson, son of Mr. and Mrs. Pliny W. Williamson, and Elizabeth M. McElroy were married on October 19 in New York City.

'01—Jane Clark Hill of Cheyney, Pa., writes: "No news. Just a steady working-away at homely, daily duties. Have three girls in college—one a senior at Oberlin. Loyalty to Alma Mater unwavering."

'02—Glenna Marie Clark, daughter of Mr. and Mrs. Arthur B. Clark (Glenna M. Hostetter) of New Haven, Conn., was married on September 8 to Robert Crafts. Mr. Crafts is a son of the late Walter N. Crafts '92 and Annie Francis Crafts ex'98. Dr. Robert E. Brown '01 officiated.

ex c'02—Mrs. William W. Taylor (Mary Wickes) and her family have recently moved into a new home on Central Avenue, Whitefish, Montana. Dr. and Mrs. Taylor's eldest son, William, is Prinicpal of the Cut Bank, Montana, High School; their second son, Robert, is a sophomore at the University of Montana; and Richard, the youngest, is a freshman in high school.

'03—Charles E. Dull is Superintendent of Science in the Newark, N. J., junior and senior high schools. He is the author of a popular high school chemistry and also a physics book published by Henry Holt & Co. His daughter, Mary Louise, is planning to enter Oberlin next year.

ex'03—Charles R. McMillen is now vice-president of the St. Regis Paper Company, Lincoln Building, New York City.

'05—Irma Miller has moved to 11419 Carolina Road, Cleveland, Ohio, where she is living with her brother, Carl (acad. '04-'05). Miss Miller is employed in the Accident Department of the Cleveland Railway Co.

'06—As Minister of the church in Deerfield, Mass., which is attended by the boys of Deerfield Academy, Harold G. Vincent enjoys meeting three Oberlin boys in school there—Charles Holmes, Charles King and Wallace Tobin.

m'07—Mary E. Moxey, Assistant Editor of the Church School Publications of the Methodist Episcopal Church, has been pegging away on the same job since 1918 (which of itself is almost news) and finding joy in its creative possibilities.

t'08—Rev. Grover L. Diehl has been transferred from the Mt. Hope Church in Detroit, Mich., to the Central Church, Dallas, Texas.

'08—Stanley B. Kent writes: "Mrs. Kent and I were in Oberlin for registration and the first day of classes, September 21 and 22. We enjoyed the rally and Frosh bonfire on Wednesday evening. Our son, Louis, is a member of the Sophomore Class."

'08—Bess Bolden Walcott transferred in September, 1931, from the high school at Tuskegee Institute, where she has been teaching English since 1918, to the principal's office as Editorial Assistant. In this capacity she is acting editor of the *Tuskegee Messenger,* director of the Tuskegee Press Service, and newspaper publicity. She is still executive secretary of the Tuskegee Institute Chapter of the Red Cross of which Dr. R. R. Moton h'15 is chairman. She finds that for the past three years this Red Cross work has been a big job all by itself. One of her major jobs is keeping house for two of her daughters, one a sophomore in college, the other in the fifth grade. Her oldest daughter is a junior at Talladega College and her son is a sophomore in the Tallahassee High School. Between times she studies Spanish, plays golf, swims and sponsors an honor club for college students.

'09—Rev. Joel B. Hayden, Headmaster of Western Reserve Academy, Hudson, Ohio, spoke on "The Eclipse of Divinity" at the Student Vespers on Sunday, November 13, in Oberlin.

'10—Edward S. Jones published an article entitled "Educational Research and Statistics" in the October 8 issue of *School and Society.*

'10—Edith Curtis arrived in San Francisco on July 12 from her missionary work in Osaka, Japan.

'10—William S. Ament is acting President of Scripps College during the absence on semester's leave of President E. J. Jagna.

'10—Mr. and Mrs. Leonard J. Christian arrived in New York on July 19 from the Mission Field in Foochow, China.

'11—Dorothy S. Blake attended summer school at Harvard University last summer, taking courses in Latin and comparative philology. "'Twas good to see other Oberlinites there, old friends and new. Among the former was Ruth Bookwalter '12, now Mrs. Arthur Hummel, whose husband was Director of the Far Eastern Seminar at Harvard last summer. I enjoyed a pleasant week-end with Grace Stewart Byrne '11 and her family in Hurley, N. Y."

'11—Helen Martin arrived in New York on September 6 after spending a year in Europe. The Carnegie Corporation have renewed her grant for another year of work, which will be taken at the University of Chicago Graduate Library School.

'12—Brigadier General C. R. Howland was transferred from command of the Fourth Brigade at Fort Francis E. Warren, Wyoming, to command of the Third Brigade at Fort Sam Houston, Texas, where he has served since March 18.

'12, '16—Willis Carl Kellogg was born on May 28 to J. Hall Kellogg and Hanna Witkop Kellogg.

'13—Mrs. Harold N. Fowler (Mary Blackford) is studying sculpture at the Corcoran School of Art in Washington, D. C.

'13—Ruth Anna Eckhart has been appointed Dean of Women at Bucknell University in the absence of Dean Amelia E. Clark. Prior to August 1 she was engaged in research work for the U. S. Office of Education in connection with the National Survey of the Education of Teachers. Her particular problem was "Current Practices in Graduate Education." Her "half-act" play, *Semper Fidelis*, appears in the October, 1932, issue of the *Personalist*.

'14—Carl W. Dipman, editor of the *Progressive Grocer*, was a speaker at the recent dedication of the largest one-story wholesale grocery warehouse in the United States at Perth Amboy, N. J.

'14—Mrs. Ada Simpson Sherwood retired from teaching at Berea College in June, 1931, and is now entering upon her second year as Church Assistant of the Union Church, Berea, Ky. She teaches a credit class in leadership training in the Church School and a class in religious dramatics in the Christian Endeavor Society. She writes occasionally for the *Congregationalist*; her most recent poem, "I Never Lose Heart," appears in the November 10 issue.

'14—Born to Mr. and Mrs. Arthur P. Honess of 210 South Allen Street, State College, Pa., a daughter, Mary Ann, on April 9.

'15—The Magazine wishes to make the following correction in the November issue: "Adrian Titterington of the Dayton Y. M. C. A." should have been Adria Titterington of the Y. W. C. A.

t'16—Rev. Frank Cary and family sailed from Vancouver on October 8 to Japan to resume their work in the Mission Field.

'17—Rudolf Hertz writes, "Have a year off! Was in Europe all summer. Returned on the *Stuttgart* with Dr. Geiser and family. I am working on my Master's degree at Teachers College this winter. My address is Apartment 77, 3120 Broadway, New York City."

'17—Mary E. Andrews, assistant professor of religion in Goucher College, attended the summer session of the American School of Oriental Research in Jerusalem, Palestine. This is one of the many distinctive features of the annual tour of Syria and Palestine conducted by Professor Arthur V. Jackson, American University, Washington, D. C. She spent two weeks in Constantinople with Eve McNaughton Markham '16, joining the group of American ministers and teachers there on July 13, and continuing with them until August 13. Independent of the tour, she spent five days in London, a week in Paris and ten days in Cairo. She recommends her summer tour to any who are interested in a summer abroad that is "different."

'17—Dorothy E. Wright is on a year's leave of absence from her work in Jersey City. Her friends will find her at 4280 Arguello Way, San Diego, Calif.

'18—Ruth Bixby is living at home in Poultney, Vermont, trying to keep her father from getting old too fast. She is also teaching part time in the Troy Conference Academy and Green Mountain Junior College.

'19—Marian W. Mair received her Master's degree from Columbia University in February, 1932. She has been teaching physical education at the State Normal School, Oneonta, N. Y., since February 1. She attended Camp Sirano, Mills College, Cal., and the Olympic Games last summer.

'19—Margrett C. Schultz is teaching Latin in the Upper Arlington High School in Columbus, Ohio.

'20—Lillian Unholz was married to J. Francis Harter on July 28 in Buffalo, N. Y. They are living at 120 Ruskin Road, Eggertsville, N. Y.

'21—"Sam" T. Burns is beginning his twelfth year as director of music for Medina County, Ohio. He taught courses in music education at the School of Education, Northwestern University, this past summer and was elected president of the Ohio Music Education Association for the year 1932-33.

'21—Glenn H. Benton received his Ph.D. degree on June 6 from the University of Iowa, where he spent the past year on a leave of absence. The subject of his dissertation was "The Politics of Thomas Hart Benton." Dr. Benton resumed his work at Drury College, Springfield, Mo., this fall where he holds the position of professor and head of the Department of History.

'22—Dorothy Alice Lee was married to Guilford L. Mack on November 10 in New York City. Mrs. Mack has been associated with the Bacteriology Department of the New York State Agricultural Experiment Station, Geneva, New York.

1k'22—Ruth Schwind is teaching second grade in the Cleveland Public Schools.

'22—Jeannette E. Dorland is a supervisor at the Cuyahoga County Child Welfare Board of Cleveland, Ohio. Address: 41 Beech Street, Berea, O.

'22—Ellen Ewing is still Librarian at Bellevue, Ohio. She was recently elected third vice-president of the Ohio Library Association. Address: 448 West Main Street, Bellevue.

ex-'22—Margaret Gail Hammaker of Lakewood, Ohio, sailed on August 9 from Jersey City on the S. S. Excalibur for Sholapur, India, where she will resume her duties under the American Board of Commissioners for Foreign Missions as a teacher in the Woronoco Girls' School.

'22—Miriam Spreng, who for the past three years has been the Visiting Teacher in the Toledo Public Schools, has accepted a position on the Visiting Teacher Staff of the San Diego Public Schools. Her new address is 3802 Center Street, the Los Altos, San Diego, Cal.

k'23, '24—David Peter Niederhauser arrived on July 15 and is still living with his parents, Mr. and Mrs. Wendell S. Niederhauser (Linda Belle McElroy), in the Danforth Apartments, Williamstown, Mass.

'23—Margaret Dann has been appointed a Sterling Fellow in physiological chemistry to work with Professor Mendel of Yale. Miss Dann earned her M.S. degree in chemistry at the University of Chicago and received her Ph.D. degree last June from the Medical College of Cornell University where she specialized in nutrition, working with Dr. Graham Lusk. Miss Dann has had six years of chemical experience with two important chemical companies and her name appears on several research publications.

'23—Helen E. Harris is teaching at the Kirk Junior High School, East Cleveland, Ohio. Address: 1745 Chapmen Avenue.

'24—Robert M. McFarland and Una Gaidry were married in Erie, Pa., on September 28. Mr. and Mrs. McFarland are at home at Park Lane Villa, Cleveland, Ohio.

'24—Margaret B. Hays took a short trip to Havana, Panama and Colombia last summer.

'24—Professor Frank L. Huntley of the Doshisha University, Kyoto, Japan, delivered a paper on "The Poetry of William Browne," a 17th century study, before the National English Literature Association of Japan at the October, 1932 meeting. The series of six volumes compiled by Professor F. Minaishi and Professor Huntley for beginners in the study of either Japanese or English, published by the Gakujido Press of Tokyo, are being used both in Japan and America.

'24—Eleanor M. Larsen lived in Paris with a French family for seven weeks last summer, and did a little work in eurhythmics at the Dalcroze School. She spent a week traveling in Switzerland and Germany before returning to Tougaloo College, Tougaloo, Miss., where she teaches hygiene and physical education.

'24, '31—Esther Robinson was born on August 9 to Mr. and Mrs. Theodore Newcomb (Mary Shipherd) of 3564 Ingleside Road, Shaker Heights, Ohio.

'25, m'31—George E. Hunsberger has been re-appointed fellow in economics at the University of Virginia where he is working for a Ph.D. degree.

'25—Mr. and Mrs. B. A. Youngs (Agnes Wells) of 100 Sound Ave., Riverhead, N. Y., have a third son, Allan Binkerd, born October 10. Their other two children are Richard, aged 3½, and Arthur, aged 1½.

'25—Helen Lehman is Assistant to the Superintendent and an instructor in the Lafayette Home Hospital, Lafayette, Indiana.

'25—Marjorie R. Jameson spent the summer on Georgian Bay, Canada. She is teaching French in the Roosevelt Junior High School, Cleveland Heights, Ohio.

'25—Ruth Mary was born on July 7 to Mr. and Mrs. Edwin R. Clark (Mary Sedgwick) of 119 Clinton Street, Fitchburg, Mass. Mr. Clark is Principal of the Fitchburg Junior High School.

'25—Elinor P. Prindle of Charlotte, Vt., is the author of a book of children's verse entitled *Polly Pringle's Jolly Jingles*. One of her poems appeared in the September *Good Housekeeping*.

'25, '25—Mr. and Mrs. Karl Prindle (Mary Rymers) of 2804 East 130th Street, Cleveland, are the parents of a daughter, Anne Barton, born September 27.

'25—Helen L. Eaton taught at Kent State College, Kent, Ohio, last summer. She is still at Marshall College, Huntington, West Va.

'25—Arthur Cassell Bates, son of Newton Bates and Gertrude Cassell Bates of the Class of '82, was married to Lillian Hodgen Hooper on June 25 in Chicago, Illinois. Mr. Bates is editor of the *Radio Amateur Call Book Magazine*, and is Ensign C-V (S) U. S. N. R. Mr. and Mrs. Bates reside in River Grove, Ill.

'25—Hazel Rickard of Medina, Ohio, spent a week in Pittsburgh, Pa., visiting Mr. and Mrs. Ralph Crandall (Lottie Pease ex'23). While there she attended the Oberlin alumni steak roast.

'26, '26—A daughter, Barbara Elinore, arrived at the home of Mr. and Mrs. Lewis E. Reark (Elinore Thatcher), 9117 Airdrome Street, Los Angeles, Cal., on September 6. Mr. Reark is Assistant District Accountant in the office of the Union Oil Company.

ex'26—Born to Mr. and Mrs. Jack M. Jessen (Nina Pancoast), 231 Bonita Avenue, Pasadena, Cal., on September 19, a son, Jack Ronov.

'26—Mary Louise Ainsworth has moved to 1250 Harvard Avenue, Claremont, California, where she is sharing an apartment with Eleanor Wilkins. "Promoted? Yes. To the position of a Sunday School teacher, as well as to active participation in normal living after repeated illness during the last few years. Married? Only to music. Still pursuing its elusive knowledge and skills."

'26—Dr. and Mrs. J. Howard McMillen spent last summer touring Europe.

'26—Mary Alice Looney was born on

June 25 to Mr. and Mrs. Lester Looney (Alma Willis) of Pelham, New York. The Looney family are enjoying the depression along with several millions more.

'26—Nothing much has happened to John Latshaw except the changing of positions—from instructorship in English at Time School, Port Deposit, Md., to head of the department of English at Hackley School, Tarrytown, N. Y.

'26, '27—Joseph Jay was born on August 28 to Mr. and Mrs. Victor Ewald (Esther Wood) of 5982 Pennsylvania Ave., Detroit, Mich. Mr. Ewald is a member of the Northeastern Y. M. C. A. staff.

ex'27—Henry R. Elster of Hammond, Indiana, was married recently to Miss Norma McCampbell of Lincoln, Nebraska.

h'27—Rear Admiral Mark L. Bristol was retired from active service in the U. S. Navy on May 1 and is now making his home at 1621 Massachusetts Ave., N. W., Washington, D. C.

'27—Virginia Van Fossan spent the month of August at the Timberline Ranch (Emily Michener ex'28 is the Ranch Director) near the White Mountains in Arizona. One of the outstanding events was a trip across the Painted Desert on horseback to see the Hopi Indian snake dances, a feature of their annual prayer for rain.

'27—Born to Lieutenant and Mrs. Roy W. Axup (Violet May Andrews) a boy, William Andrews Axup, on October 3 at Fort Hayes, Columbus, Ohio.

'27—Elizabeth Snyder is having a busy time as music instructor in charge of the orchestra, band and some choral classes in the new Arsenal High School of Pittsburgh, Pa. She also has an organ position at the Shields Presbyterian Church in a suburb of Pittsburgh.

'27—Margaret Noss has started her fourth year as science teacher in the Hollidaysburg, Pa., High School.

'27—Clinton W. Root recently published a paper concerning temperature and light intensity of luminous bacteria in the *Journal of Cellular and Comparative Physiology*.

'27—Dr. and Mrs. Paul H. Reed (Grace Good) announce the birth of their son, Robert Allen, on August 21 at Texhoma, Okla.

'27—John B. McKelvey has joined the Research Staff of the Industrial Rayon Company. His address is 3326 Bosworth Road, Cleveland.

'27—Leona E. Massoth attended the International Conference of Social Workers at Franklin Am Main, Germany.

'27, '28—Born to Mr. and Mrs. William M. McCord (Evangeline Andrews) of 1328 Jackson Avenue, New Orleans, La., a son, James Andrews, on July 1.

k'27, '28—Nelle Irene Graham and Dr. Chandler M. Brooks were married on June 25. Dr. Brooks holds a National Research Fellowship in physiology at the Harvard Medical School.

'28—Elsa Carlson is teaching again at the Geneva, Ill., Community High School.

'28, '29—Margaret Brooks and Richard Schaefer were married on August 20 in the First Church, Oberlin, Ohio. They are now living at 381 Front Street, Berea, Ohio.

m'28—S. C. Wang is teaching at the

National Central University in Nanking, China.

'28—Alfhild Johnson is still with the Rockefeller Institute for Medical Research in New York. She was transferred in June from the department of Dr. Correl to that of Dr. Leslie T. Webster who is working in the field of experimental epidemiology. She has her own apartment at 214 East 51st Street, Apt. 1E, and would be glad to see Oberlin friends at any time.

'28, m'32—Wallace S. Baldinger received an Institute of International Education scholarship and spent the summer of 1932 studying history of art at the Institute of Art and Archaeology, University of Paris, as part of a two-summer course in candidacy for the diploma offered at the end of that period—"Brevet d'Histoire de l'Art de la Sorbonne." He is at present Director of the Art Department of Washburn College and associate professor of history and appreciation of art.

'28—Harold C. Jones was married to Alice Alden Drew on April 29 in Pasadena, Cal. Mrs. Jones is a graduate of Pasadena Junior College and a member of the California Junior College Honor Society. Mr. Jones is working for his Ph.D. in botany at the Nebraska State University. Their trip from Pasadena in June "was an extended honeymoon through very picturesque parts of the Southwest. It took us into the Grand Canyon—that Mecca of natural beauty—and past Pike's Peak, the land-mark of the plainsmen." They are at home at 1223 H St., Lincoln, Neb.

c'28—Elizabeth Stuart is teaching piano, organ and harmony in Redfield, S. D.

'28, '29—The birth of Shirley Anne Webster was officially announced on August 31. If this is not known soon at Oberlin she will be announcing the historic fact herself. Her parents are Mr. and Mrs. Robert D. Webster (Arline Flach).

'28—Rev. Emmett P. Paige has been Rector of St. John's Episcopal Parish in Poultney, Vermont, since September 15.

'28, '29—Sara J. Jones and William B. Tucker were married in Oberlin, Ohio, on October 29.

'28—Mr. and Mrs. William R. Landles announce the birth of a daughter, Jean Marilyn, on August 6.

c'28—Mr. and Mrs. Hugh P. Williamson spent last summer at the Seagle Colony, Schroon Lake, N. Y., where Mrs. Williamson received her study of voice with Oscar Seagle and Mr. Williamson taught piano and theoretical subjects. Mr. Williamson has recently returned to his work as Dean of Music at Flora Macdonald College, Red Springs, N. C., after a southern concert tour with Elsa Zimmerman, Contralto.

'28, '30—Dr. George L. Evans and Annette M. Church were married on September 3. Dr. Evans is spending six months at the Boston City Hospital "trying to learn some neurology."

'29—The engagement of Ruth Wagener, a member of the University of Wisconsin Class of 1933, to Dr. Alfred W. Downes has recently been announced. Alfred received his Ph.D. degree in August and now holds a post-doctorate associateship at the University of Wisconsin.

c'29—Frances K. Beach was married on June 15 to George S. Carlson in Bristol, Conn. Mr. Carlson is connected with the Bristol Bank and Trust Company. Mrs. Carlson is the organist and choir director at the First Baptist Church in Waterbury, Conn., and has her own studio in Bristol. Address: 24 Woodland Street, Bristol, Conn.

'29—Katherine Love is employed in the Children's Department of the Bloomingdale Branch, New York Public Library.

'29—Nineteen hundred and thirty-two again finds Margaret I. Bane teaching English and dramatics in the Connellsville High School, Connellsville, Pa. She attended the full summer session at Chicago University last summer where she is working for her Master's degree. She advocates much travel to Chicago next summer to attend the World's Fair.

c'29—Eunice Kettering is studying at the School of Sacred Music, Union Theological Seminary, New York City. Her address is 99 Claremont Avenue, New York City.

c'29, '32—Mr. and Mrs. William F. Ashe Jr. (Marjorie Richards) are living at 1782 East 101st Street, Cleveland, Ohio. Mrs. Ashe is working for the Cleveland Associated Charities and has discovered that there are lots of poor people. "But," she adds, "so are we." Mr. Ashe finds his first year in the Western Reserve Medical School lots of work and lots of fun.

'29—Janet Winchester is director of music and education in the First Presbyterian Church of Lansing, Mich. She tells us that her chief disappointment in Lansing is that "there are very few Oberlinites on the local map."

'29—Mr. and Mrs. P. C. Michel (Dorothy Hope) have moved from Schenectady, New York, to 289 Norton Street, New Haven, Conn. Mr. Michel is doing graduate work in electrical engineering at Yale University.

'30—Karl J. Hinnerschietz spent the latter part of last season in Allentown, Pa., as director in the Civic Little Theater. He is now engaged in the Theater Guild's production of *The Good Earth.* His address is 100 Haven Avenue, New York City.

'30—Following is an excerpt from a letter written by the mother of Hollis W. Barber: "He is spending fifteen months in Germany. He won a German-Ameri-

can exchange fellowship to study in the University of Berlin. He went to Munich for summer school. Then he wandered through the Rhine Country, visiting several such cities as Heidelberg, Rothenberg, Cologne, Gottingen. While in Gottingen he stayed in the home of a delightful and cultured retired Admiral whose specialty during the War was placing torpedoes where they would do the most harm—an interesting experience for a student of international relations." Address: bei Frau Regierungsrat Joel, Berlin—Friedenau, Kaiserlee 135, Deutschland.

c'30—Mr. and Mrs. James A. Rose (Lucille Frye) of 17 Webster Place, East Orange, N. J., announce the arrival of a daughter, Ann Elizabeth, on August 21.

'30—G. M. ("Red") Lawrence was married on August 30 in Norwalk, Ohio, to Nellie May Andrews, a graduate of the Ohio University Kindergarten-Primary School in 1928. Mr. Lawrence is teaching science in the Crestline High School. Address: 301 Clink Blvd., Crestline, Ohio.

ex'30—David Stratton Shields was born on May 28 to Mr. and Mrs. James H. Shields (Ruth Stratton) of 210 Wooster Avenue, Mt. Vernon, Ohio. Ralph W. Stratton '05 and Elsie Hull Stratton c'05 of Norwalk, Ohio, are the proud grandparents.

'30—Lawrence C. Ross spent last summer touring Europe. On a sightseeing tour of London he had the unexpected pleasure of accidentally meeting Oberlin's newlyweds, "Larry" Kiddle '29 and Mrs. Kiddle (Allene Honglan '30). They were on their honeymoon. Mr. Ross is teaching at West High School in Rochester, N. Y.

c'30—Thomas W. Williams is teaching in the fast growing music school at Dakota Wesleyan University. Voice, elementary harmony and directing (University band, University School Chorus and the local Philharmonic Civic Chorus of two hundred voices in the presentation of Bach's Christmas Oratorio) keep him busy, extremely happy and single.

'30, '30—Marian Arnold and Kenneth W. Miller were married in Wethersfield, Conn., on July 2. Previous to her marriage Mrs. Miller was engaged in family welfare work for the charity organization in Hartford, Conn. Mr. Miller is still with the Providence Community

Fund and at present is extremely busy with the campaign. They are at home at 392 Benefit Street, Providence, R. I.

'30—Harriott B. Churchill has turned musical with a vengeance. She was one seventy-fifth of the chorus in San Diego's annual community outdoor play, *Heart's Desire*. She is a member of "Polyphonia," an a cappella choir organized by the former director of the Kansas City Conservatory, and is occupying a chair in the alto section of one of the church choirs. Her major is ecology!

'30—K. Eugenia Noble is supervising the school paper and teaching mathematics in the Blume High School, Wapakoneta, Ohio.

'31—George W. Harwood took a year's graduate work at the Ohio State University in the School of Social Administration. At the present time he is associated with the Syracuse, N. Y., Community Chest and Council as Campaign Secretary of the Community Chest Drive.

'31—Donald T. Dixon has been taking care of his father's insurance business since the first of May. Donald hopes to get a broker's license and make the insurance business his "life work."

c'31—Lawrence S. Frank is working toward the degree of Master of Music in Theory at the Eastman School of Music, Rochester, New York.

c'31—Margaret Kluge attended the summer school of Juilliard in New York City, studying piano with James Friskin and advanced keyboard harmony with Howard Talley. On August 8 she played *Etude*, Op. 25, No. 3, by Chopin and Liszt's *Waldesrauschen* in a public recital. After completing her work at the summer school, she played in a trio at Hotel Marseilles on Broadway. She has recently returned to her work at Morningside Conservatory, Sioux City, Iowa, where she has six seniors in piano, sixty new children in piano classes and supervises teaching.

c'31—Phillis M. Keeney has the same position—teaching school music in Buffalo—and enjoys it more than ever.

'31—Kathryn Ruch was graduated from the Katharine Gibbs School of New York City last May, and in June accepted a position as private secretary to an attorney. Her address is 45 Tiemann Place, New York City.

'31—Jared H. Ford is attending the University of Illinois this year. He is doing graduate work in organic chemistry as well as being a part-time freshman chemistry teacher.

'31—J. N. Stannard tells us that Harvard University looks like a miniature class reunion for the classes of '31 and '32. He finds that the great number of Oberlinites around Boston make life very pleasing and friendly. His new work and new surroundings are, so far, as nearly perfect as one could expect in the year of our depression, 1932.

'31—F. Naomi McFarland is back again this year in Monroeville, Ohio, where she is teaching Latin and English in the High School. She is also sponsoring two different classes, a Latin Club and coaching plays. "Last and best," she writes, "I am engaged to John A. Neubauer '30. He is at New York University working on his Master's degree."

'31—Elizabeth ("Biz") Reeder is again instructor in physical education for women at the University of South Dakota, Vermilion, S. D.

'31—Grace E. Kline is teaching 160 freshmen and sophomores the difference between "ain't" and "have not" in their mother-tongue. Her address is 291 Thew Avenue, Marion, O.

'31—Mary Elizabeth Nelson, daughter of Charles A. Nelson '89 and Jennie Elmore Nelson ex'95, was married on November 5 to Ellery Denison in Canton, China. Mr. Denison is associated with the Chase Bank in Honkong.

'31—Joseph W. Meriam acad. '95-'00 and Florence Wiley Meriam c'06 of Shaker Heights, Ohio, announce the engagement of their daughter, Elizabeth, to Roderick McLellan Grant of Oak Park, Ill. Mr. Grant is a graduate of Beloit College, Beloit, Wis., where he was a member of Beta Theta Pi.

'31—Mary F. Bosshart is teaching the pre-school group in the Brush Hill School, Milton, Mass., and is living at South End House in Boston. She finds Boston a regular Oberlin colony.

'31—William H. Prigmore is still employed by R. G. Dun & Company as a traveling reporter.

'31—John G. Grau is enrolled at the University of Chicago Medical School. His "best treats so far have been meeting former Oberlin friends on the Campus."

'31—Dorothy L. Butler is working in the library and teaching two French classes in Southern Union College, Wadley, Ala.

'31—John Grindley is a medical student at Harvard University.

'31—What has happened in 1931-32? Marjorie Watters advises us to ask the politicians! She continues: "After one year of moping and writing letters and having interviews, I decided the word NO made up 85% of the words now in use. And so I am going to school some more in Dayton, Ohio—taking a secretarial course and is it fun! Also during this year of idleness I've learned a hundred and one things that may come in handy in the next fifty years. If any of the Oberlin family should come down my way—do drop in. I'll guarantee that there will be no depression talk."

k'32—Marion Bell has enrolled in the School of Education of Western Reserve University.

k'32—Susan Bratton is studying at Beaver College, Jenkintown, Pa.

'32—Dorothy Niehus is teaching physical education at the Van Cleve School, Dayton, Ohio.

k'32—Frieda Schmude has entered Michigan State Normal College at Ypsilanti, Mich.

k'32—Sarah Carnahan is teaching second grade in the Oberlin, Ohio, schools.

k'32—Ruth Chaffee is teaching in Mantua Township, Portage County, Ohio.

k'32—Harriet Collen has a kindergarten position in Maumee, Ohio.

k'32—Ethel Finley is teaching the first and second grades in the Parkman, Ohio, schools.

k'32—Carrol Fretz is teaching kindergarten in the Institution for Feeble Minded, Columbus, Ohio.

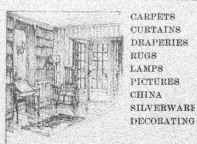

Lightning Source UK Ltd.
Milton Keynes UK
UKHW021144061218
333419UK00013B/2178/P